The Decasections

of Life

The Ultimate Manual For Living The Balanced Life

Wole Olarinmoye

WORD2PRINT
A Division of One-Touch UK

THE DECASECTIONS OF LIFE

Copyright © 2014 Wole Olarinmoye

Scriptures are taken from the Holy Bible, New Living Translation unless otherwise stated.

First published in the United Kingdom in 2014 by Word2Print
www.word2print.com
ISBN: 978-1-908588-10-4

A CIP catalogue record for this title is available from the British Library

Printed and bound by CPI Group (UK) Ltd, Croydon, CR0 4YY

Table of Contents

Dedication

To my late parents Joseph Olajide and Victoria Ebunoluwa Olarinmoye who believed in the wisdom that God has given me. I know you would have been filled with pride. You are always in our thoughts.

Preface

If there was ever a book I have wanted to write, this would be it. This is what I want to be remembered for. My life, my work, my beliefs, my focus, all culminate in the word: balance.

As a teenager growing up in the church setting, I was very aware of various inferences to various phrases like 'your Christian life', or 'your work life' or 'your marriage life'. I learnt from then, that as individuals, we all have many 'lives' all competing for attention, struggling for emphasis in a busy world. I consider myself a bit of a philosopher, and as I started to study life as a whole and the people around me, I came to the conclusion that broadly speaking we could split our lives up into at least 10 sections. Hence the term 'Decasections' was coined. *Deca* is from the Greek word for 'ten' and sections- **the 10 sections of life.**

Although the concept of the Decasections was initially developed to help me manage and ensure balance in my own life, I discovered through my observations and studies that many people sacrificed one or more areas of life for success in another leaving them successful and miserable. I discovered that certain aspects of life were very easily overlooked but an individual is unlikely to feel complete, fulfilled or even happy unless all the aspects of what I refer to as a balanced life are present.

All in all, is it really worth it; being successful but miserable? I started to use the truths I had learnt in my own life in mentoring others and found that it provided an easy means of reference to check on how one was doing in life. At times of crises, it helped me to remain thankful as I appreciated that life was not as bad as it seemed if only one area was failing and all the others were doing well.

In many respects this book is my take on life as seen through my understanding of the word of God and my many years of experience observing people as a General Practitioner (GP).

The Decasections of Life will help you understand the various 'lives' you are living and how each one contributes to making you a complete person. It will help you assess what is important to you and also enable you to keep things balanced in your life. It will not provide you with all the answers you need for every area of life but it should stimulate you to want to search and develop more, about whatever area you feel you are currently deficient in. Each chapter has a few questions at the end to help you crystallize what you have learnt and also what you need to do to move forward.

In addition to this there are many questions in this book. The aim is to drive you to meditation, introspection and reflection with a view to growth. Don't just read the questions; spend time discovering the answers which will make your experience richer.

It is my prayer that you will stand perfect and complete in all the will of God for your life in Jesus name.
Enjoy and God bless!

Wole Olarinmoye
London, July 2014

Acknowledgments

I thank the Almighty God for the wisdom, desire and ability to write this book. Lord, without You I would not have been able to do this. Thank You.

I also thank my darling Dami for her invaluable support, suggestions and advice towards the preparation of the manuscript. You are my wife, girlfriend, mistress, best friend, confidant, counsellor and adviser. I will always love you. I thank my children who have encouraged me to finish the work and are a constant inspiration to me. Guys, you are absolutely the best!

I also thank the leadership of New Wine Church, London especially the late founding pastor Dr Tayo Adeyemi and the current senior minister Pastor Michael Olawore. A lot of the material for this book came from the messages I preached in church. Sirs, thank you for the opportunity to be a blessing to God's people and now the world.

I thank Muyiwa Olumoroti who kept encouraging me to write a book even when I did not think I had it in me. Brother, may your tribe increase in Jesus name! I also thank Kemi Oyesola whose skilled editing has made this book the success story that it is. Sister, may the Lord bless you real good.

My sincere appreciation goes to family members, friends, work colleagues, church members; you have all contributed to making me who I am. May the Lord bless you and protect you, may He smile on you and be gracious to you, may He show you His favour and give you His peace in all the Decasections of your life in Jesus name.

DECASECTION

One

SPIRITUAL

The most important area of your life is your spiritual life. So we will look at this first. Man is primarily a spirit being. In John 4:23-24 the Bible says

> But the time is coming—indeed it's here now—when true worshipers will worship the Father in spirit and in truth. The Father is looking for those who will worship him that way. For God is Spirit, so those who worship him must worship in spirit and in truth."

The only way to acceptably worship God is in spirit and in truth. God is a spirit and He made us in His likeness so we are spirits. We also have a mind and a body but as we are made in the likeness of God, we are primarily spirits. If the Bible says that God is looking for true worshipers who will worship Him in spirit and in truth then our primary obligation in life is to honour God who created us. Matthew 6:33 says

> Seek the Kingdom of God above all else, and live righteously, and he will give you everything you need.

Note the phrase 'above all else'. God wants us to seek

1

His kingdom above all else. The primary thrusts of our lives should therefore be spiritual.

As we start to discuss our spiritual lives, we need to be clear that this refers to our spiritual walk with God, primarily our personal connection with God not our work for Him in church. Remember that as we are first spirit beings, God expects us to grow in our spiritual experience. We may all be at different levels in our Christian walk but we all need to keep developing ourselves spiritually.

Taking this a little further, I want you to note the expression 'true worshipers' from the passage in John chapter 4. If there are true worshipers, that means there are also false worshipers. In order to grow in our spiritual experience we need to know what makes us true worshipers. When we know what makes us true worshipers, we would know what the true spiritual life consists of; then, it would not be rocket science to understand that developing those areas, walking more and more in those areas will ensure that we grow spiritually.

So what makes you a true worshiper? Is it the fact that you attend church regularly? Is it the fact that at one time in your life you answered an altar call; is that what makes you a true worshiper? Is it because you have been baptised by water immersion or even because you serve as a worker in your local church? Is it because you believe that Jesus is Lord? Is that what makes you a true worshiper? What is it that makes you a true worshiper? Let me give you the answers to these questions.

Are you a true worshiper because you attend church? Obviously not. Church attendance is important but that's not what makes you a true worshiper. The Bible tells us that when the sons of God gathered in Heaven, the devil was there amongst them and God addressed him, you can see that in the book of Job chapter 1.

Are you a true worshiper because you believe in God? A big NO. James 2:19 says

> You say you have faith, for you believe that there is one God. Good for you! Even the demons believe this, and they tremble in terror.

Are you a true worshiper because you serve in church? Oh NO! Matthew 7:22-23 says

> On judgment day many will say to me, 'Lord! Lord! We prophesied in your name and cast out demons in your name and performed many miracles in your name.' But I will reply, 'I never knew you. Get away from me, you who break God's laws.'

Remember we are discussing about growing spiritually and understanding what makes us true worshipers. So what is it that makes you a true worshiper? At least four things.

The first is this: You are a true worshiper because the Word finds expression in your life.

There must be a manifestation of God's word in your life. Matthew 7:17-21 says

> A good tree produces good fruit, and a bad tree produces bad fruit. A good tree can't produce bad fruit, and a bad tree can't produce good fruit. So every tree that does not produce good fruit is chopped down and thrown into the fire. Yes,

just as you can identify a tree by its fruit, so you can identify people by their actions. "Not everyone who calls out to me, 'Lord! Lord!' will enter the Kingdom of Heaven. Only those who actually do the will of my Father in heaven will enter.

There must be evidence in your life that the word of God is producing fruit. There must be an expression of God's word and God's will in your life. If you claim to have a spiritual experience but there has been no change in your personal walk and relationship with God, no change in character, no longing to do the will of God, I encourage you to question your being a true worshiper. Hebrews 4:12-13 says

> For the word of God is alive and powerful. It is sharper than the sharpest two-edged sword, cutting between soul and spirit, between joint and marrow. It exposes our innermost thoughts and desires. Nothing in all creation is hidden from God. Everything is naked and exposed before his eyes, and he is the one to whom we are accountable.

A true worshiper voluntarily exposes, subjects and submits his or her life to the scrutiny of the word. The word must be at work in you, dividing the soul and spirit, reaching down to expose the thoughts and motives of your heart, making you naked in the sight of God. The most important area of your life is your spiritual life. The word of God is supposed to strip away the layers. If you have not subjected your life to this level of scrutiny by the word I encourage you to question your being a true worshiper. In James 1:19-27

> Understand this, my dear brothers and sisters: You must all be quick to listen, slow to speak, and slow to get angry. Human anger does not produce the righteousness God

4

desires. So get rid of all the filth and evil in your lives, and humbly accept the word God has planted in your hearts, for it has the power to save your souls. But don't just listen to God's word. You must do what it says. Otherwise, you are only fooling yourselves. For if you listen to the word and don't obey, it is like glancing at your face in a mirror. You see yourself, walk away, and forget what you look like. But if you look carefully into the perfect law that sets you free, and if you do what it says and don't forget what you heard, then God will bless you for doing it. If you claim to be religious but don't control your tongue, you are fooling yourself, and your religion is worthless. Pure and genuine religion in the sight of God the Father means caring for orphans and widows in their distress and refusing to let the world corrupt you.

The word has said it all. Don't just listen to God's word, you must do what it says, then God will bless you for doing it. Being a true worshiper involves putting into practice the truth of the word of God. Joshua 1:8 says

Study this Book of Instruction continually. Meditate on it day and night so you will be sure to obey everything written in it. Only then will you prosper and succeed in all you do.

Why meditate in the word? Why read the word? Why come to church to listen to it? That you may be sure to obey all that is written in it. If you don't have a resident decision in your heart to try and practice ALL of God's word, I encourage you to question your being a true worshiper.

What else makes you a true worshiper?

The second is this: You are a true worshiper because you

5

live a life of Worship, praise and thanksgiving.

Ephesians 5:18-21 says

Don't be drunk with wine, because that will ruin your life. Instead, be filled with the Holy Spirit, singing psalms and hymns and spiritual songs among yourselves, and making music to the Lord in your hearts. And give thanks for everything to God the Father in the name of our Lord Jesus Christ. And further, submit to one another out of reverence for Christ.

Colossians 3:16-17 says

Let the message about Christ, in all its richness, fill your lives. Teach and counsel each other with all the wisdom he gives. Sing psalms and hymns and spiritual songs to God with thankful hearts. And whatever you do or say, do it as a representative of the Lord Jesus, giving thanks through him to God the Father.

A true worshiper lives a life of worship, praise and thanksgiving irrespective of what he or she is going through. If you do more of complaining and whining than worship and thanksgiving, I encourage you to question if you really are a true worshiper. The Bible says we should examine ourselves on a daily basis. 2 Corinthians 13:5 says

Examine yourselves to see if your faith is genuine. Test yourselves. Surely you know that Jesus Christ is among you; if not, you have failed the test of genuine faith.

Whatever you are going through learn to give God

thanks and praise, learn to worship. The scripture we read in Ephesians above said we should endeavour to have regular praise and worship sessions deep down in our hearts. For some of us those songs will be modern and contemporary, for others the songs will be more traditional. It doesn't matter what you are singing, just sing to the Lord.

By constantly complaining and murmuring the children of Israel limited and grieved God. They always had something to grumble about. Now don't get me wrong, stuff happens and we don't always understand why, but the Bible says in everything give thanks. That is the mark of a true worshiper.

Many years ago, my wife Dami and I were expecting a baby. Unfortunately Dami suffered an abruption at 39 weeks which means the placenta separated from her womb before the baby was born. This led to us losing the baby but also put Dami's life in danger. Her blood pressure went up significantly and she had to be started on medication. It was a very painful experience, especially for Dami, as many of her friends were also pregnant around the same time and they all had their babies with little incident.

As painful as the experience was, we chose to give thanks and worship God. We applied the Decasections of Life, and realised that although we were unhappy with the way things were in one area of our life, we could see the faithfulness of God in so many other areas. It was not easy but we did. We reckoned that God could cause all things to work together for our good. We kept up our church commitments, we strengthened and encouraged those around us who were distraught at what happened to us and we maintained our worship, praise and thanksgiving. Several things happened as a result. So many people who had other challenges in their lives changed their disposition and attitude and became more thankful and appreciative to God. Women who had challenges in the area of child bearing or pregnancy saw Dami as a source of encouragement and with her background experience of previously working as a midwife, a ministry of encouragement to women which she still has today was born. She eventually came off medication and to cap it all off God blessed us with a beautiful baby girl. Glory to God!

A true worshiper will develop and grow in Worship, praise and thanksgiving. It is an attitude of faith knowing that God is able to cause all things to work together for you. (Romans 8:28). You can achieve so much more in your life by having the right attitude: Trust God and praise Him even when things don't seem like they are adding up.

The third is this: You are a true worshiper because you Walk in the Spirit.

Galatians 5:25 in the New King James Version says

If we live in the Spirit, let us also walk in the Spirit.

To live in the Spirit means to be alive to God and to spiritual things. The Bible is saying if we are alive to God and to spiritual things then let us also walk in the Spirit. The New Living Translation says

Since we are living by the Spirit, let us follow the Spirit's leading in every part of our lives.

Walking in the Spirit means following the leading and guidance of the Holy Spirit in every part of our lives.

Galatians 5:16 says

So I say, let the Holy Spirit guide your lives. Then you won't
be doing what your sinful nature craves.

The New King James Version says

I say then: Walk in the Spirit, and you shall not fulfil the lust
of the flesh.

Romans 8:14 says

For all who are led by the Spirit of God are children of God.

These scriptures tell us something very clear. A true
worshiper, one who lives in the Spirit, will also walk in the
Spirit; allowing the Holy Spirit to lead and guide every area of
the person's life. This will result in the true worshiper living
above the inherent
sinful nature also
known as the lusts
of the flesh. This is
extremely important
as God hates sin and

> *The most important
> area of your life is your
> spiritual life.*

sin interferes with our relationship with God. Sin is falsehood
and our worship must be in spirit and truth. There is another
reason why we must seek to walk in the Spirit. 1 Corinthians
2:9-12 tells us

That is what the Scriptures mean when they say, "No eye
has seen, no ear has heard, and no mind has imagined what
God has prepared for those who love him." But it was to us
that God revealed these things by his Spirit. For his Spirit
searches out everything and shows us God's deep secrets.
No one can know a person's thoughts except that person's

own spirit, and no one can know God's thoughts except God's own Spirit. And we have received God's Spirit (not the world's spirit), so we can know the wonderful things God has freely given us.

From this passage we can see that God has prepared special and wonderful things for those who love Him but the revelation of those things come to us by the Holy Spirit. The Bible goes on to explain that we have received God's Spirit so that we can know the wonderful things God has freely given us. This agrees with the function of the Holy Spirit as explained by Jesus in John 16:12-14:

There is so much more I want to tell you, but you can't bear it now. When the Spirit of truth comes, he will guide you into all truth. He will not speak on his own but will tell you what he has heard. He will tell you about the future. He will bring me glory by telling you whatever he receives from me.

The Holy Spirit is in our lives to guide us into all truth and also to tell us about the future! We do not need to live our lives in the dark, the Holy Spirit can guide us into the things God has freely made available for us!

So how can we practically experience the guidance of the Holy Spirit? Let me use this analogy. The realm of the spirit is like the internet. There is a lot of information waiting to be accessed and downloaded. The Holy Spirit is like your broadband provider. There are various connection levels and speeds based on your level of investment to the broadband service. Your spirit is like a laptop. It can function to a certain level without the internet but is infinitely more resourceful when it has its Wi-Fi settings on, AND is logged into a good broadband provider which is connected to the internet.

In learning to walk in the Spirit, you need to learn to understand how your spirit is 'feeling' at every point in time. The 'feelings' of your spirit are the downloaded packages received from the realm of the Spirit which your spirit has to interpret. Some people refer to these feelings as 'hunches'.

Many years ago on a Christmas afternoon, my brother and I wanted to go and visit my sister. As we drove out of our compound, I had a very strong uncomfortable feeling in my spirit that something was not right. I tried to pray if off but it remained very strong. I chose to ignore it. As we drove along, I kept trying to shrug off the feeling but it wouldn't go. We didn't get to my sister's house that day. We were stopped by policemen about two miles to her house and kept by the roadside for about six hours. (We did not have the car's documents on us.) The annoying thing was that my sister was not even at home! She was at a church program and only after the program had finished could she come and plead with the policemen and we were eventually released. We got home that night at 11pm having left home in the early afternoon and being stuck at a police-check point for 6 hours. On later reflection, I realised my spirit was warning me of the impending situation but I did not understand. Walking in the Spirit can save you from danger because the Holy Spirit knows all things.

A true worshiper will develop walking in the Spirit. This will ensure living above natural desires that lead to sin, and also enjoy the benefits and blessings of the guidance of the Holy Spirit.

The fourth is this: You are a true worshiper because you are at War with the devil.

In one way or another, in the way you live your life, in your service to God, you should be at war with the devil. If there is nothing you are doing on a regular basis to actively and aggressively push back the kingdom of the devil from your life or that of the people around you then I have to encourage you to question your being a true worshiper of God. Psalm 149 says

Praise the Lord! Sing to the Lord a new song. Sing his praises in the assembly of the faithful. O Israel, rejoice in your Maker. O people of Jerusalem, exult in your King. Praise his name with dancing, accompanied by tambourine and harp. For the Lord delights in his people; he crowns the humble with victory. Let the faithful rejoice in that he honors them. Let them sing for joy as they lie on their beds. Let the praises of God be in their mouths, and a sharp sword in their hands — to execute vengeance on the nations and punishment on the peoples, to bind their kings with shackles and their leaders with iron chains, to execute the judgment written against them. This is the glorious privilege of his faithful ones. Praise the Lord!

From this scripture it is clear that if you are a saint of God, a true worshiper, then you have the honour of doing two things; rejoicing and praise seen in the first six verses which we have already looked at under worship, praise and thanksgiving as well as war and fighting against the enemy. The Bible says this honour have ALL the saints not some but all. As a true worshiper, as a saint of God you are expected to challenge the enemy, execute judgement on the enemy, punish the enemy, restrict his operations in your own sphere of influence and ensure that God is glorified. 1 John 3:8 says

> But when people keep on sinning, it shows they belong to the devil, who has been sinning from the beginning. But the Son of God came to destroy the works of the devil.

As the body of Christ we have the same purpose Jesus had which is to destroy the works of the devil. Now we will all do this in different ways, in different places based on our different callings and different spheres of influence but the point is if we are true worshipers of God then we should be at war with the devil. Isaiah 41:15 says

> You will be a new threshing instrument with many sharp teeth. You will tear your enemies apart, making chaff of mountains.

God sees you as an instrument of war in His hands through whom He can bring judgement on the works of the devil. Every time you stand for righteousness, every time you serve in your local church or charity with the right heart, every time you spread the good news of Jesus, every time you cause glory to be given to God, you are attacking the kingdom of darkness.

Every time you visit the sick, feed the hungry, give godly advice or counsel, rescue someone from a wrong pathway you are counteracting the works of darkness. Anytime you do something that opposes the devil you reflect your being a true worshiper. In addition to this you should be living a life of intercession. Practice the art of praying regularly for the people around you, your family members, friends, leaders in church, co-workers, colleagues at work, neighbours. Remember that whatever you sow, you will reap. Galatians 6:7-10 says

> Don't be misled — you cannot mock the justice of God. You will always harvest what you plant. Those who live only to satisfy their own sinful nature will harvest decay and death from that sinful nature. But those who live to please the Spirit will harvest everlasting life from the Spirit. So let's not get tired of doing what is good. At just the right time we will reap a harvest of blessing if we don't give up. Therefore, whenever we have the opportunity, we should do good to everyone — especially to those in the family of faith.

So how can we be true worshipers? From these points we can see that we are true worshipers when the Word finds expression in our lives, when we practice lives of Worship, praise and thanksgiving; when we Walk in the Spirit in every area of our lives and when we regularly engage in War to destroy the works of the devil.

Similarly we could ask the question; how can we progress spiritually? By growing in the Word, increasing in Worship, developing our Walking in the guidance of the Holy Spirit and becoming stronger in spiritual Warfare.

So from time to time, pause and ask yourself: Is the Word still finding expression in me? Am I still living a life of Worship, praise and thanksgiving? Do I Walk in the Spirit in every area of my life? Is my life still being used by God as an instrument of War against the devil?

John 3:16-17 says

For God loved the world so much that he gave his one and only Son, so that everyone who believes in him will not perish but have eternal life. God sent his Son into the world not to judge the world, but to save the world through him.

We can only effectively become true worshipers through a relationship with Jesus. God gave Him as the ultimate sacrifice for our sins. He did not come into the world to judge it but that through Him we can be reconciled to God. No other religion deals with the paramount problem of sin. Sin must be dealt with. No matter how good a person has been, if a DNA test convicts them of a crime committed 20 years earlier, the person will still go to jail. Only accepting Jesus as Lord and Saviour wipes away your sins because Jesus has already paid the price. I encourage you today to accept Jesus as Lord and Saviour, to re-establish your connection with God, to become a true worshiper.

If you want to do so, pray this prayer from your heart:

Dear Lord Jesus, I accept that I have sinned. I also understand that all wrong doing must be punished. I thank you for taking my place and accepting the righteous punishment of God on my behalf. I believe you died on the Cross to set me free from eternal punishment. I confess my sins and I forsake them from today. I decide to live for you and become a true worshiper by ensuring the word of God finds expression in my life, living a life of worship, praise and thanksgiving for all you have done for me and also playing my part in the war against the devil. In Jesus name I pray.

15

If you prayed this prayer genuinely from your heart, why not write to me via my website *www.decasections.org* and let me know and I can help support you in your new found faith and decision to be a true worshiper.

Once you have genuinely connected yourself to God, you have to invest in this Decasection of your life on a regular basis. Whatever you do not invest in will depreciate and deteriorate. Begin to actively read and study the word of God. Learning to read the word of God regularly with a view to practicing what you read will enable you to develop your spiritual walk with God.

1 Peter 2:2-3 says

> Like newborn babies, you must crave pure spiritual milk so that you will grow into a full experience of salvation. Cry out for this nourishment, now that you have had a taste of the Lord's kindness.

You must crave the spiritual milk of the word of God so that you can grow into the full experience of salvation. Actively and consciously live a life of worship and thanksgiving to God. Actively ensure that the devil does not have his way in your life or the lives of the people around you.

As we come to the close of this chapter, this is the time to ask ourselves two questions:

RIGHT QUESTIONS, RIGHT ANSWERS

1. Why is this Decasection important?

The most important area of your life is your spiritual life. Without a connection with God you are at risk of losing out on eternity. You can only effectively become a true worshiper through a relationship with Jesus.

2. What must you do to invest in this Decasection of your life? Whatever you do not invest in will depreciate and deteriorate.

You must read the word of God regularly and practice what you read. You must actively and consciously worship God and live a life of thanksgiving to Him. You must oppose the devil and give him no room in your life. You must associate and be with other believers and bear fruits by winning others to the Lord.

DECASECTION

Two

PURPOSE

After your spiritual life the most important area of your life would have to be your purpose. Ephesians 2:10 says

> For we are God's masterpiece. He has created us anew in Christ Jesus, so we can do the good things he planned for us long ago.

What is purpose? It can be defined as the 'raison d'etre' or the reason for being. The one truth I want you to take away from this chapter is that everyone has a purpose. Many books have been written on purpose and I will not attempt to give you a complete dossier or analysis on purpose in one chapter. However I want to help your thinking and refine your thought process when you consider purpose.

Ephesians 2:10 says we are God's masterpiece! Think about that for a moment. God spent time on us, creating us, designing us, putting us together for a purpose. So when we consider purpose, we are essentially saying we were designed for a reason. There is a reason for instance, why you have your abilities, your personality and your experiences. They all feed into something; God gave them to you. Your purpose is the reason you exist. That means you will be at your best and feel most fulfilled when you are walking in it. Your purpose is ingrained in you, it is who you really are before you were damaged (sorry, influenced!) by society.

I was twelve when I started to open up to my purpose. I was sitting in church one day towards the back of the auditorium on the right side of our small church building at the Foursquare Gospel Church, Lagos Island in Nigeria. As I sat there, I could not help thinking that I wanted to be in a position to give people good advice. I looked around me and saw people from different walks of life and I had a strong feeling that made me feel like I wanted to help them. I knew I was only 12 years old. I also knew I did not know what I could to do to help them but I wanted to be in a position to. That was over 30 years ago. Now all I do is help people and give them good advice either through my profession as a General Practitioner or through my standing as one of the leaders in my church community. I am constantly helping people by giving them good advice.

Now along the way I have had to train, study and develop myself. I have had to learn to understand people but at the age of 12 I had an inkling of what I should be doing, what would make me feel most fulfilled. That experience is not unique to me. Many children before they are damaged (sorry, influenced!) by society have deep-seated dreams and aspirations but unfortunately those dreams and aspirations are never fulfilled. They grow up instead chasing money, sexual experiences, fame/power and perpetuate the cycle of unhappiness associated with our world today.

Parents have a big role to play in helping a child fulfil their purpose. Proverbs 22:6 says:

> Direct your children onto the right path, and when they are older, they will not leave it.

You must direct your children onto the right path. There is a right path for every child. You cannot and should not paint all children with the same brush. Every child needs to be treated as an individual and it is the responsibility of every parent to set their child on the straight and narrow path that leads to purpose.

The discovery and pursuit of purpose guides you in the choices you make, the friends you keep and the things you do. An individual with the future in mind is less likely to be cavalier about life than one who is living for today.

Why is the discovery of Purpose important?

We have established the fact that we are not here by chance or as the result of an accident. So it goes without saying that if we are created, born or designed for a reason then living our lives outside of that reason is a waste of time. Life is short and while you may not be thinking of eternity, the truth is that the more time you spend doing irrelevant things, the less time you have for your true relevance.

Myles Munroe a preacher from the Bahamas said, 'If the purpose of a thing is not known abuse is inevitable.' If you don't know why a thing exists, you are more likely to misuse it. You will accept your own ideas for its existence, you will accept other people's ideas for its existence, you will accept even the devil's idea for its existence. Likewise if you don't know why you exist, you are more likely to abuse your life with negative pursuits such as drugs, alcohol, illicit sex or maybe even good pursuits which are completely irrelevant to your purpose.

Let me give you a simple example. If I have a nice, brand new Ferrari, red in colour with large alloy wheels and right in the middle of the road I had a breakdown, how do you think I will feel? Upset, frustrated? The car still looks beautiful, it still has great alloy wheels, it is still shiny red but I will be upset and frustrated because the primary purpose of the Ferrari is not just to look pretty but to

> *The discovery and pursuit of purpose guides you in the choices you make*

take me from A to B. In life, there is nothing wrong with being pretty, rich, educated or well-known as long as all those things are accessories of purpose rather than being your main focus. If they are your focus you will end up feeling frustrated with life. If fame or money was the answer, why do some celebrities live such unhappy lives? Why do they need alcohol or drugs to keep them going? This gives us a very important key to life: Frustration and being constantly upset could be a very strong indicator that you are out of sync with your purpose.

Let me give you five reasons for discovering your purpose.

1. **Knowing your purpose gives meaning to your life:** Direction. Your life now has a curriculum with which to run. You know you are going somewhere; you have a career rather than a job. You focus on certain things and not others. It helps

you to decide which direction to go in life.

2. Knowing your purpose simplifies your life: No excesses. Instead of trying to do everything or running helter-skelter you hone in on the important things that are necessary to help you get to where you are going in life.

3. Knowing your purpose focuses your life: No distractions. This is similar to 'simplify', you are able to concentrate on doing certain things even if you don't particularly like them, you purposely avoid distractions that will pull you away from your purpose.

4. Knowing your purpose motivates your life: Goal. There are times you will feel tired, worn out, fed up and maybe something has gone wrong. Purpose is what sustains your motivation in life.

5. Knowing your purpose prepares you for the eternity: Reward We must never forget that Purpose is not just about this life and this earth. The Bible tells us all our works will be tested by fire and those that stand will be rewarded but those that don't will have nothing to show for all their activity on earth.

Having looked at some reasons for discovering purpose, let us now look at what I call the three elements to Purpose which you need to be very clear about. The list can be further expanded but three are absolutely essential. I will phrase them in questions that you must repeatedly ask yourself and seeking the answer will lead you on the path to self-discovery and eventually purpose.

1. WHO AM I?

There are many people that can be referred to as 'you'. We have the 'you' at work that your colleagues know, the 'you' at home that your family knows and the 'you' at the club where you play tennis, go swimming or use the gym. We even have the 'you' that regularly attends church or some other place of worship. But who are you really? Or maybe a more apt question is: who are you supposed to be? Actually both questions are relevant. 'Who are you' asks in relation to your current identity while 'who are you supposed to be' asks in relation to your actual identity.

While you may appear to others to be a happy go lucky, friendly, responsible married woman, you may actually be a deeply troubled, broken victim of sexual abuse whose marriage is on the verge of collapsing because issues from the past have not been adequately dealt with. However, maybe you are supposed to be a strong spiritual Christian who has handed over her past to the Lord, walking in forgiveness and is now using her experience to strengthen and encourage others. Can you see what level of introspection just asking this question can open? You should be asking yourself this question on a regular basis: Who am I?

Now for the hypothetical woman that I have described above, answering the question 'who am I' will see her start to open her past history of sexual abuse and unhappiness in her marital home. Notice though that those are situations and circumstances that have happened to her, but who she is has nothing to do with what has happened to her! Likewise who you are has nothing to do with what has happened to you.

You are God's masterpiece created for good works!

Take a lion for instance. You can shave his mane, trim his claws and lock him in a cage; he won't stop being a lion because those things have happened. So when asking yourself the question 'who am I' or maybe more relevantly 'who am I supposed to be', you need to strip away the happenings, the disappointments, the situations and the circumstances and look deep into your inner being, your heart, your spirit and your soul. You need to dig deep beneath the surface to see what you were and are supposed to be before you were damaged (sorry influenced!) by the happenings of life and society and ask the question: who am I? When you start to see the question in this sense then 'who am I' and 'who am I supposed to be' become one and the same question.

The direct, plain and general answer to the question is that you are God's masterpiece, created for good things. The details and specifics can only be found out by communicating with your Maker.

There are however a few pointers which may help you to start to focus in the right direction. I will introduce this by giving some examples first. We discussed about a Ferrari earlier on. Based on the fact that it has four wheels you don't need the IQ of a rocket scientist to know it is supposed to move a person from one place to another but beyond this, as a result of how it looks, it is supposed to do this in flamboyant style. However if you look at a truck which also has four wheels but in addition it has a very large container behind it, you can guess that it is supposed to move big or heavy items from one place to another. In the case of a truck, flamboyance and style are completely irrelevant.

Likewise by looking at the equipment in a room, you can tell what the room is used for. Take for example a room that has a lot of seats, all facing in one direction, audio speakers arranged around the room with an amplifier at the back. Obviously that room is a meeting room. A room in your house that has a reading table, office type chair, books on shelves and a computer is obviously a study. Another room has cupboards, a microwave, cooker; that room is a kitchen. The point is from the type of equipment an object possesses you can tell what it was designed for or equipped to do. Likewise by looking at your 'equipment' we can have some pointers as to who God wants you to be.

There are five types of equipment to consider when talking about purpose. They form the acrostic **SHAPE.** This is an acronym for Spiritual gifts, Heart, Abilities, Personality, Experiences. You can read more about this in Rick Warren's book Purpose Driven Life but I will delve into it briefly here.

1. **Spiritual Gifts** refers to spiritual abilities given to you by God

2. **Heart:** What makes you mad, sad or very glad? What are your motivations, interests, desires, inclinations?

3. **Abilities:** What are your natural abilities? Do you have a flare for music, sports etc?

4. **Personality:** What is your character type? There is no right or wrong character. God will use all people of different character types for different purposes. Are you:

- *Sanguine?* They are: Cheerful, friendly, talkative, lively, restless, the life of the party

- *Choleric?* They are: Optimistic, active, confident, strong-willed, aggressive

- *Melancholic?* They are: Sensitive, analytical, a perfectionist, unsociable, moody

- *Phlegmatic?* They are: Calm, dependable, efficient, easy-going, passive, stubborn

Note that most people have a mixture of personality types rather than being all of one or another.

5.   **Experiences:** All experiences, positive or negative can become tools in God's hands to be used for His glory.

Romans 8:28 says:

And we know that God causes everything to work together for the good of those who love God and are called according to His purpose for them.

You are the best person to answer all these questions and engage in the whole process. It will take time, reflection, introspection and meditation but you will start to develop the answers and discover who you really are.

2. WHAT SHOULD I BE DOING?

Very closely associated with who you are is what you should be doing. Let us look at Ephesians 2:10 again.

For we are God's masterpiece. He has created us anew in Christ Jesus, so we can do the good things he planned for us long ago.

The Bible says God created us in Christ Jesus so we can do. We are created to do. God will not create you to do something He has not equipped you to do. As we start to discover who we are, we will also start to realise that along with who we are is what we are to do.

Just as we all have a purpose, we have all been equipped with gifts, graces, abilities, talents and experiences that we should be using to God's glory. We explored this at the end of the last section when we were dealing with who we are. God intends you to use the gifts you have been equipped with for His glory.

Paul told Timothy in 2 Timothy 1:6 to activate his spiritual gift.

> This is why I remind you to fan into flames the spiritual gift God gave you when I laid my hands on you.

'Fan into flames' refers to developing and utilising your gift, grace, talent or ability. Everyone has something that makes them unique. One of my late pastors (Dr) Tayo Adeyemi of New Wine Church London taught the world to discover, develop and deploy their gifts. There is something you do better than most of the people around you. That in itself may be a clue to what you are supposed to be doing. When you assess yourself and have discovered what gifts, abilities, inclinations and talents you have, you should start to develop them and deploy them for God's glory.

I have told you the story of how I felt from the age of 12 that I should be giving good advice. I soon discovered that I have an ability to analyse situations, reflect on them and draw out potential life theories about situations and circumstances.

28

By testing these theories in my own life and that of others, I developed pertinent life lessons which I could pass on to others.

> *God will not create you to do something He has not equipped you to do.*

Armed with a strong knowledge of the word of God, medical knowledge and life experiences I started to fulfil my deep desire of giving people sound advice and pointing them in the right direction.

3. WHERE SHOULD I BE?

I believe there is a place in life where you add the most value. There is a place in life where you are at your most productive. I call it the principle of Divine Location. This concept applies to where you live, where you work, where you worship, where you express your abilities but most importantly where you carry out your purpose. Let me explain: any crop growing in an unwelcome environment will not thrive. Anything that grows away from its intended place is dangerous. A cancerous cell is a cell that has overstepped its boundary and is growing and multiplying elsewhere.

In life I have seen people take steps to relocate geographically i.e move and start living in another place and their lives have become significantly worse while there are others whose lives have become better. The yardstick is not in how much money they made from relocating but actually how their lives turned out. Drawing examples from the Bible, the first man Adam was comfortable and fulfilled when in the

Garden of Eden. Everything he needed and wanted came to him there; his career, his wife; everything was well with him until he left the garden.

There is a place where you add the most value. Abraham was asked by God to leave the land where he was, to move to a land where God would bless him. The land he was moving to was his divine location. As long as he remained there, things went well and if you read the story of Abraham, things went bad for him when he left the land of promise.

Abraham's son Isaac also wanted to leave his divine location in Genesis Chapter 26. The Lord told him to stay even though the environment was unfavourable but we see that Isaac was blessed and fulfilled despite the adverse conditions. There is a place where you are supposed to be.

The principle of Divine Location states that God does not bless you where you are; God blesses you where you are supposed to be. Fulfilment will not come to you where you are; fulfilment will be waiting for you where you are supposed to be. I believe that if you are serious about fulfilling purpose, you need to ask yourself the question, 'where should I be'?

Many years ago shortly after I qualified as a GP, I was working in a lovely surgery about five minutes' drive from where I lived. I was being paid more than I had ever earned and I paid off all my debts apart from my mortgage. After morning surgery I would go home, sleep or do other things and then go back to work for evening surgery. It was a dream life. However deep down in my heart I knew something was not quite right. I felt dissatisfied and unfulfilled. One day in a night prayer meeting, in the lower auditorium of my church at the back I felt so strongly that I should go to Dartford and look for a job there. I had always felt that was where the Lord wanted me to be but now I felt the time was right. I did and God blessed me with a locum job at Temple Hill Surgery. I eventually became one of the General Practice principals there which is another testimony in itself. I believe this place is my divine location as God has blessed me there with wonderful colleagues and a great working environment where I feel at home. My work there is more of a ministry as I help and support my patients through personal issues way beyond medical practice or treatment.

Where should you be? Do you feel like you don't belong where you currently are? Do you feel like a fish out of water at work or church? Then maybe you should be seeking God to find that place where you belong and where you can add the most value.

I cannot finish this section without discussing the leading of the Holy Spirit. The Holy Spirit has been given to us to help us live the Christian life. I like referring to Him as my own personal Jesus.

John 14:26 says

But when the Father sends the Advocate as my representative—that is, the Holy Spirit—he will teach you everything and will remind you of everything I have told you.

Jesus refers to the Holy Spirit as His representative. Look at what 1 Corinthians 2:9-12 says

That is what the Scriptures mean when they say, "No eye

has seen, no ear has heard, and no mind has imagined what God has prepared for those who love him." But it was to us that God revealed these things by his Spirit. For his Spirit searches out everything and shows us God's deep secrets. No one can know a person's thoughts except that person's own spirit, and no one can know God's thoughts except God's own Spirit. And we have received God's Spirit (not the world's spirit), so we can know the wonderful things God has freely given us.

The Holy Spirit wants to reveal to us the things that God has prepared for us. Look at verse 12. It says there are certain things God has freely given to us. We were not meant to struggle in life. We are supposed to find peace, joy and fulfilment by being who God wants us to be, doing what God wants us to do and being where God wants us to be.

Now why is it important to fulfil purpose? There are at least three reasons.

The first reason is direct and simple. You are God's masterpiece created to do good things. If that is the case, then you should discover what God designed you for and do the good things he created you to do. The second is a bit more frightening. All our works will be tested by fire. This is how 1 Corinthians 3:11-15 puts it.

For no one can lay any foundation other than the one we already have—Jesus Christ. Anyone who builds on that foundation may use a variety of materials—gold, silver, jewels, wood, hay, or straw. But on the judgment day, fire will reveal what kind of work each builder has done. The fire will show if a person's work has any value. If the work survives, that builder will receive a reward. But if the work is burned up, the builder will suffer great loss. The builder will be saved, but like someone barely escaping through a wall of flames.

All our works will be tested. If they don't stand the test of God's fire then it will be destroyed. Only the work that has been built with the right materials will stand. First we must be sure we are building what God wants us to build but also that we are building with the materials He wants us to build with. Our work for God must not be done for reasons of personal gain or pride but for the glory of God.

To explain the third let us look at the following passages of scripture.

Then I said, 'Look, I have come to do your will, O God — as is written about me in the Scriptures. *(Hebrews 10:7)*

Thank you for making me so wonderfully complex! Your workmanship is marvelous — how well I know it. You watched me as I was being formed in utter seclusion, as I was woven together in the dark of the womb. You saw me before I was born. Every day of my life was recorded in your book. Every moment was laid out before a single day had passed. How precious are your thoughts about me, O God. They cannot be numbered! I can't even count them; they outnumber the grains of sand! And when I wake up, you are still with me! *(Psalms 139:14-18)*

And I saw a great white throne and the one sitting on it. The earth and sky fled from his presence, but they found no place to hide. I saw the dead, both great and small, standing before God's throne. And the books were opened, including the Book of Life. And the dead were judged according to what they had done, as recorded in the books. *(Revelation 20:11-12)*

"I knew you before I formed you in your mother's womb. Before you were born I set you apart and appointed you as my prophet to the nations." *(Jeremiah 1:5)*

From the scripture in Hebrews 10 we read that Jesus clearly stated that His life had been written out for Him in a book. Some of you will say that book is the Bible and maybe it is, maybe it isn't. But from the passage in Psalms you can see David also saying that his life has been written out for him in a book before he was born. Look at Ps 139 verses 16 and 17. Now that's definitely not the Bible. Revelations 20 also shows that we will all be judged according to certain books that will be opened on the last day.

Let me tell you what I believe from these scriptures: there is a library in Heaven that has a book or books that has recorded everything you are supposed to accomplish. David got a glimpse of that book and said "Wow! The thoughts of God for us are precious, too many to count."

This means your purpose is pre-ordained and this is confirmed by what we read in Jeremiah. God knew us before we were born and had pre-planned our purpose. (We have already established that we are God's masterpiece). This means that you can only fulfil purpose when you take hold of what has been written concerning you and walk in it. This means that you will be judged based on how much of what has been written in that book you have accomplished. This means that your life has a marking scheme. This means that what you consider to be important may or may not be relevant to the marking scheme of

> *There is a place in life where you are at your most productive.*

your life. This means that you may or may not have been wasting your time so far on earth. This means that WE ALL have some serious praying, meditation and reflection to do. Why? There is a marking scheme for our lives.

This Christian life just got easier and harder all at the same time. You want to know your purpose? Find out from the Holy Spirit (your link to God) what is written about you in that book from the library of heaven and do it. Nice and easy; but easier said than done.

As we come to the close of this chapter, this is the time to ask ourselves two questions.

RIGHT QUESTIONS, RIGHT ANSWERS

1. Why is this Decasection important?

This decasection is important as it will help to keep us on the straight and narrow path of life and fulfilment. Walking in purpose also determines what reward we will get in eternity. We will only be rewarded for doing what we should have done. Getting things right in the area of purpose ensures you are fulfilled. You get to understand who you are, what you should be doing and where you should be in life.

2. What must you do to invest in this Decasection of your life? Whatever you do not invest in will depreciate and deteriorate.

If that sounds too far-fetched, ask yourself these simple questions: Who am I? (Who am I supposed to be?) What should I be doing? Where should I be?

As you start to develop your answers, the picture of your purpose will get clearer and clearer. The Holy Spirit will guide you into His truth and you will step into your fulfilment in Jesus name.

DECASECTION

Three

PROFESSION

Your profession can be defined as what you spend most of your working hours engaged in. Some people work as doctors, lawyers, pastors, nurses, dentists, engineers, receptionists, technicians, and plumbers. The list is endless.

Your profession is an extremely important area of your life as you spend at least (for most people) a third of your whole day and about half of your waking hours at work. For many people, if you factor in travel time, it is well over half. For this reason your profession should be much more than just a job. A job is what you do simply to make money to get by and pay the bills. You spend way too much time at work for it just to be a place you struggle through day after day.

In an ideal world, you should be able to express significant aspects of your purpose in your profession. Your purpose is what you were created to do, what you will be judged by in eternity; your profession is what you spend your most productive hours and years doing. Should they not be one and the same or at least, very closely related? If your purpose is where you find fulfilment, then the more time you spend engaging in it, the better. Unfortunately, we have many people who have their purpose as hobbies and then drag themselves through the daily grind of jobs they hate and cannot wait to get out of. A very unhealthy state indeed.

Choosing a career path is one of the most important decisions in your life. In my opinion, after your decision to get saved by giving your life to Christ and the decision if to marry or who to marry, your career choice probably ranks as one of the top decisions you will be faced with. Many are stuck in career paths they ended up in rather than chose as they felt left with little or no alternative.

Although it is never too late to do what is right for you, the best time to make a good career decision is very early, usually about the second or third year of secondary school at the latest. The reason for this is that the diversification of subjects starts soon after and knowing where you want to end up in life helps you to determine what you should be doing.

Picking, Pursuing and Progressing in Your Profession

When you think of the future, what do you see? What would you like to be doing? As mentioned above your profession should be very much linked to your purpose. What are you interested in that will earn you a decent wage and allow you to live a comfortable and fulfilled life?

There are usually two extremes when dealing with picking a career. If you ask some young boys from certain neighbourhoods in London what they see themselves doing, many of them will give you answers like 'I want to be a DJ' or 'I am a footballer'. While these are well paying professions the overall success rate is very poor and the failure rate is extremely high. I do not discourage people from pursuing dreams but I do encourage people to be realistic about their prospects for life in a chosen field. If you are pursuing a high risk profession like those mentioned above and at this stage I should probably include acting or singing as well then please have a back-up plan to avoid being stuck on a path with no future prospects and no alternatives.

The other extreme is one in which the only professions that exist on earth worth doing are professions in the medical, legal, engineering or accounting fields. Now the truth is: many parents ask their children to pursue careers in these fields as you can guarantee a measure of success and responsibility in those who pursue such careers. Most doctors, lawyers, engineers or accountants are comfortable, responsible members of society who are able to look after

> *You spend way too much time at work for it just to be a place you struggle through day after day.*

and provide for their families. However, it is also important to note that we all have varying interests and are not all very academic. I believe it is important that a child is allowed to pick their career but it is also equally important that they are given the right guidance to enable them to do so. If you are one of those who has found themselves in a career you did not really choose it is never too late to do the right thing. The question is: "what would you rather be doing?"

Lack of fulfilment is a killer! It can destroy and tear people apart if left unchecked. In order to compensate, people then start to involve themselves in various unprofitable activities, seeking artificial highs which deepen the mire they find themselves in. However if you see lack of fulfilment for what it really is: your inner self telling you 'I am more than this', then you can channel that energy into positive change. If you feel unfulfilled in your profession then it is time to change to something you are interested in where you will find fulfilment.

There are certain things to consider in determining if a professional path or career is the right one for you. You can also use these questions to determine if a particular job opportunity is the right one for you. I have phrased this as five questions.

1. Would it pay you what you feel you are worth?

We all have a measure of self worth. If we are being paid less than what we feel we are worth, we would still feel unfulfilled, feel used and feel frustrated. Whatever work we do should value us enough to pay us what we are worth. Having said this we must be realistic about what we are worth.

Many years ago while working for the employment service, my sister came across a young man who was upset at the job offers he was getting from the Job Centre. He was refusing to attend certain job interviews and when challenged by my sister his answer was, 'would you take up a job that paid you peanuts?' My sister almost felt sorry for him until she looked through his file and saw that he was a school drop out with no qualifications.

Unfortunately in today's job market your value is based on what you have to offer society. If you do not have much to offer, then your market value or worth will be deemed to be low but if you do have a lot to offer, then your market value or worth will be deemed to be high. So while you should have a healthy self-worth, you should also have a realistic self-worth.

Romans 12:3 says

Because of the privilege and authority God has given me, I give each of you this warning: Don't think you are better than you really are. Be honest in your evaluation of yourselves, measuring yourselves by the faith God has given us.

You can increase your self-worth by developing yourself educationally or by improving yourself vocationally. We are not all academically inclined so educational development may not apply to us all but remember you have to have something to offer society or you will not be valued in the job market. You might be a sports person, a tradesman or a businessperson so improve your skills, be better than your peers, stand out from the crowd; let the quality of your merchandise speak for itself. While you will always be valuable in the sight of God and your family, your earning potential is determined by what you have to offer society.

2. Would it allow you to be a true worshiper of God and walk in purpose the way you are designed to?

We have mentioned that your career should be closely linked to your purpose. If what you do interferes with your relationship with God or prevents you from expressing and fulfilling your purpose then that cannot be the career for you. The Bible says in Matthew 6:33:

Seek the Kingdom of God above all else, and live righteously,

41

and he will give you everything you need.

Seeking God's kingdom should be our first priority. We should do this through the lives we live, through the company we keep and through the jobs we do. Many years ago when I first arrived in London, I had to pass a certain exam as a foreign graduate which qualified me to work as a doctor in the United Kingdom. While looking for work most people I came across told me I could only get work outside London. At the time I was a very important member of a small but impactful community church that would have missed my commitment if I had to work away from home. I prayed, asking God to provide a job for me that would still allow me to fulfil my responsibilities to the Kingdom of God through the church where I believe God had planted me. By God's grace I never had to work away from home.

The principle of Divine Location as explained in the chapter on Purpose is in operation here. If you are where you should be then things will fall into place for you. Remember that God blesses you where you are supposed to be not where you are, which is why throughout scripture you see examples of people who did not fulfil destiny until they were located where God wanted them to be. If your chosen job or career path means you always have to miss out on meeting with God's people or not being able to fulfil your Christian responsibilities then be careful that it is not leading you astray even if you are being well paid.

Now the proviso to this is that certain professions like doctors or nurses need to be on duty at the evenings and weekends but this is usually varied and should not completely interfere with your God inspired commitments.

3. Would it allow for time with family and friends?

As important as your profession or career is, it is absolutely crucial that it should not rob you of time to spend with friends and family. Nobody on their death bed wished they could work longer hours, close one more business deal or earn more money. The regret of most people as they fade away from this life is wishing they had spent more time with family and friends. So to avoid that regret, ensure your profession or career allows you that time for healthy relationships. Ignoring this principle has jeopardised many marriages, contributed to the absent father syndrome and fragmentised family relationships.

I am very wary of jobs and careers which mean one spouse is in a different location from the other for long periods of time especially when children are involved. This has led to countless affairs, improper conduct, mistrust and divorce. Many children have grown up not knowing their parents even though they live under the same roof. Many parents have realised too late that their precious children were under the influence of some bad 'eggs' in society as they were too busy to notice the breakdown in communication.

One of the benefits of the Decasections of Life is that it allows you to reflect on your whole life and see what might be suffering if you are not paying attention to it. Some jobs and careers are so demanding that in themselves may not allow for time with family and friends. This is when to consider part-time working. Many professional women and some men work part-time or reduced hours. They have prioritised the family and work fewer hours to ensure their spouses and children are not neglected. I recommend that professional women who are very family inclined should work part-time. For one reason the difference in pay for most people when taxes, nursery or child minder fees are factored in is very small.

When our children were young, we found Dami, (my wife) was better off working part time because once nursery fees, travel costs and other expenses associated with running a house when working full time were factored in, she was only gaining £100 each month and we found it more productive for our marriage and family, and much less stressful for her to work part time.

I have had this same conversation with many working mothers in my surgery who are stressed with trying to juggle jobs/careers, young children, husbands and a fading social life. I have challenged some of them to sit down and do the maths. Most of them find they are better off working part-time than working full time and gaining one or two hundred pounds more a month with all the attendant stresses and pressures. Obviously I would always recommend that the couple agree on whatever plan of action they choose to take and not all circumstances are the same but the point is, as important as the profession is, it should not rob you of time for your friends and family.

4. Would it allow for career progression and development?

Certain jobs have been referred to as having glass ceilings. This is a term meaning that although there is a theoretical potential for progress, there is no actual progress available. One of the things you must assess in any career or job path is the opportunity for progress. Once the novelty of getting a job wears off you want to know that you can move forward, that there will be opportunities for progress and the possibility of promotion. You want a place that will allow you to express your creativity, develop other skills and abilities and showcase your talents. A well paying job with no future prospects will lead to boredom, depreciation and stagnancy. A less paying job with good prospects will lead to innovation, skill development and increased confidence.

5. Will it lead you to where you want to get to in life?

Everyone should have a vision of where they want to end up in their careers. It is your goal, your focus, your zenith. Is this career path or job taking you there? There are at least two things to consider here. There is the aspect of what you want from the job such as value, fulfilment, financial reward, responsibility and all the other things we have mentioned above. There is the other aspect of being positioned strategically in society to reflect the light of God and be the salt of the earth. Matthew 5:13-16 tells us about being the salt of the earth and the light of the world:

> You are the salt of the earth. But what good is salt if it has lost its flavor? Can you make it salty again? It will be thrown out and trampled underfoot as worthless. "You are the light of the world — like a city on a hilltop that cannot be hidden. No one lights a lamp and then puts it under a basket. Instead, a lamp is placed on a stand, where it gives light to everyone in the house. In the same way, let your good deeds shine out for all to see, so that everyone will praise your heavenly Father.

Salt in old times was used as a preservative for food. By nature, things go bad if left to their own devices. As the salt of the earth you preserve your environment and prevent things from going bad. Someone once said all that is required for evil to flourish is for good men to do nothing. As the salt of the earth you can stand for righteousness in your sphere of influence.

Light provides illumination. As the light of the world you are to reflect and radiate God's glory so people will have a good testimony of God and of Christianity. God wants to you to be established in your profession so that you can be salt and light for Him in your society. Your profession is not just your means of earning, it is God's tool for placing you right at the heart of society to preserve His values, reflect His character and radiate His glory.

> *Lack of fulfilment is a killer!*

There are seven potential spheres of culture and influence identified which have been called the Seven Mountains of Culture. This refers to Arts & Entertainment, Business, Education, Family, Government, Media, Religion. This direction of thought aims to highlight a very important fact. The light of a Christian is not needed primarily in a church setting. Light is needed most where there is darkness. God wants us as true worshipers to shine our light in the society where it is needed most. Your profession, your expertise is the means by which God plants and positions you in society to make impact for Him. You may not be listened to because you profess to be a true worshiper of God but they will listen to you because you are their financial adviser, their lawyer, their doctor or even their secretary.

The body of Jesus was removed from the cross and buried by men of influence in the society at that time, Joseph of Arimethea and Nicodemus. Men like Joseph, Nehemiah and Daniel were all men of influence in their various secular environments, and their influence benefited the kingdom of God. Your influence can benefit the kingdom. Your profession is a tool in God's hands. It is not unimportant, it is not insignificant. It is crucial you find where you fit in so that you can glorify God through your career. We will discuss each of these areas briefly to give some insight into what is required when pursuing a career in those areas of culture.

Arts & Entertainment: The prominent careers here would be acting and singing. This area is traditionally one kept away from by true worshipers of God. The potential for immorality is high in the Arts and Entertainment industry but God is looking for sound people who can shine the light of Christ in these areas.

Business: The prominent careers here would be financiers, stockbrokers and investment bankers but also any self employed business or trades persons. Although the business world is full of corruption, God is looking for honest men and women who will refuse to be corrupted but will instead uphold the values of morality in a decaying society.

Education: The prominent careers here would be the traditional learned professions of teaching, medicine and law. These fields deal with constant learning and transmission of information. We all remember the good teachers we had when we were younger. This is a place where we can impact the children as they grow up and leave them an example to follow. At a point in their lives many children value what their teachers say above that of their parents. If God had godly teachers in place to challenge the children to live godly lives from a young age, that would impact society positively.

Family: The major profession here is that of parenting and this also includes 'stay-at-home' parents. The fabric of society has been damaged by the loss of traditional family values. Co-habiting, sex before marriage and the resultant effect of children born out of wedlock has resulted in an increase in dysfunctional children from dysfunctional homes. Add to that the trauma of divorce and the pain that children especially, but also men and women have been through and you have a melting pot for breeding all the ills in society. God is looking for all of us to uphold the values of family by the lives we live but also by our influence in society.

Government: This includes all forms of political office. Many Christians are trying to form Christian political parties that uphold Christian values. A more effective way would be for Christians to belong to main stream political parties and work to influence policies and decision making. The major pitfall of politics is that many get sucked into the mire and become no better than the people they set out to change but God still needs people like Joseph, Esther and Daniel who through their careers and influence reached the higher political offices and made a difference for God.

Media: The prominent profession here is Information Technology. Everything now has a media undertone or aspect to it. Influence in the area of media is needed to help propagate the gospel in places where it needs to be heard and received. While preparing this script my friend and editor informed me about a training session he held highlighting the tactic of the media which is to influence what people hear, see, think and do. They tend to manipulate, control, dictate and influence; and if the right people do not get involved in media, the wrong people will be free to propagate whatever they want with no counter message.

Religion: The prominent professions here are that of the five-fold ministry of Apostle, Prophet, Evangelist, Pastor and Teacher (of the word of God). Unfortunately many members of the five-fold ministry have left a lot to be desired. In-fighting, quarrelling and rebellion have resulted in the proliferation of churches. The leaders of the Church and those who have been called to the mountain of religion need to live exemplary lives in order for society to take notice of what we are doing. If there are as many religious scandals as there are political scandals, what example are we setting?

The Ideal Worker

There are certain characteristics that qualify you as an ideal worker. We have discussed about professions, careers and jobs but certain characteristics will serve you well irrespective of what field you find yourself in. We have all encountered that person who you would rather not work with but we have also encountered that person whom you are delighted has been placed in your team. Who is the ideal worker? According to a study of employers there are five characteristics of the ideal employee. With each characteristic I have mentioned a few points to explain them.

1. Dependability: Works to a high standard consistently, attends work regularly, not going off sick.

2. Honesty and Integrity: This is more than telling the truth but includes working to a good pace, not wasting time, not using office supplies personally, not creating errors for others.

3. Proactive, positive attitude: Cheerful, respectful, and helpful.

4. Willing to work: Good work ethic, manages change well, handles conflict and leadership maturely.

5. Uses down time productively: Personal development, innovation, personal organisation.

In summary we have discussed a check list of five things to assess any career or job opportunity that comes your way. We have also seen the seven mountains of culture where God wants to position us to be salt and light for him. Finally we have looked at five characteristics of the ideal worker so that we can realise it is not just about the job but also about how we approach our work. I know of people who attend church asking to be prayed for as they keep losing their jobs. When you take a closer look, they are not dependable, they lack integrity and they have bad attitudes. They don't want to work and they are lazy. Prayer is not

> *Seeking God's kingdom should be our first priority.*

what they need, they need character development. No matter how 'Christianly' they are, there is little hope for them in the employment sector. See how Psalm 11:3 puts it:

> When the foundations are being destroyed, what can the righteous do?

RIGHT QUESTIONS, RIGHT ANSWERS

1. Why is this Decasection important?

This decasection is important as the most productive hours of our day and years are spent working at our professions. We need to align our professions and purposes to ensure we are at our most productive. Understanding the 5 questions of professional progress and fulfilment, the mountains of culture you have been sent to and the characteristics of an ideal worker will further help to drive you in the right direction.

2. What must you do to invest in this Decasection of your life? Whatever you do not invest in will depreciate and deteriorate.

Regularly ask yourself the 5 questions of professional progress and fulfilment to see where you are.

Are you working towards being the Ideal Worker?

Have you identified the mountains of culture you are called to?

Four

PHYSICAL

Your body is your permission to live on earth. If you look after your body, your body will look after you. The body has been designed by God to repair itself; so many, unfortunately, do not treat their body well and expect it to still function as normal. A lot of illnesses are preventable and so we are going to focus on what you can do to be in the best possible state of health. This is important as if you are ill, you will not be in the best position to fulfil your purpose or your career. Even simple things like playing with the children can become strenuous.

The numbers game

When a person is very ill, many of us are aware that there are certain indices or numbers referred to as vital signs which provide a measure of 'how alive' a person is. These are the pulse, temperature, blood pressure, respiratory rate, Glasgow Coma Scale and so on. For a person who is not particularly ill, measures of wellness, not of illness are more useful. For such an individual some of the vital signs may not be particularly applicable (such as the Glasgow Coma Scale, respiratory rate and the temperature). The others like pulse rate, blood pressure along with more indices of wellness like BMI (Body Mass Index), blood sugar and blood cholesterol provide an indication of a person's health status. Changes in these values are usually the first signs that a person may be heading down in the direction of illness even though they still feel well in themselves.

I used to give advice to anyone who was either approaching or over the age of forty to be familiar with their numbers. In recent times I have lowered that age to thirty five and maybe even thirty. When I was in medical school, it was said to be almost impossible for people to have high blood pressure before the age of forty unless there was a specific cause. Now, almost twenty years later, high blood pressure in people under the age of thirty has become increasingly common. Life is so much more stressful and the food we eat is so much less natural, making it important that we keep an eye on our bodies to ensure it is doing what we want it to do and also what it is supposed to do. You will notice that as we go along, all these parameters are only ever expressed as numbers; and often health promotion campaigns are tagged 'Do you know your numbers?'

I will discuss each of these important numbers briefly in turn and what we can do about improving them.

Blood pressure

This is a function of your cardiovascular health. In the western world Ischaemic heart disease is the number one cause of death. Your blood pressure measures the pumping action of your heart and also the resistance of your arteries to that pumping action. The normal blood pressure is usually given as a set of numbers 120/70 for example. The upper reading is your systolic blood pressure which is a function of the pumping action of the heart. It is said to be low if less than 90 with symptoms and high if greater than 140 irrespective of symptoms. The lower reading is your diastolic blood pressure which is a function of the resistance of your arteries to the flow of blood through them. It is said to be low if less than 60 and high if greater than 90.

If you check your blood pressure and your readings are outside of 90-140/60-90 then you should seek medical advice EVEN IF YOU FEEL WELL. Typically raised blood pressure does not cause symptoms unless there are other associated problems. Remember the indices being discussed here are not indicators of illness but of wellness. If they are outside of the normal range, you may not be ill but you are not well either.

In 90-95% of people there is no cause found for raised blood pressure and is therefore know as Primary Hypertension or Essential Hypertension. However, although there is no detectable cause, associated factors such as stress, increasing age and family history are implicated. Blood pressure is important as it is a major factor in heart attacks and strokes. In fact it is a significant predictor of these illnesses and of sudden death.

As mentioned above, if your readings are outside of the recommended range you should seek medical advice. Exercise is an important factor in lowering blood pressure but we will discuss this later.

Pulse rate

Closely associated with your blood pressure is your pulse rate. This is a measure of how fast your heart is beating. The effects of the beating of your heart is transmitted through all the arteries in your body and this can be felt in certain specific points where the artery is superficial enough to be felt such as the carotid pulse in the neck, the radial pulse in the wrist. Others are the brachial pulse in the elbow, femoral pulse in the groin and the dorsalis pedis pulse on the foot.

A lot of medical information can be gleaned from the pulse but only two things are of great significance to us: the rate and the regularity. The normal heart or pulse rate of an adult is usually expressed as a number per minute and usually ranges from 60-100 per minute. The lower your rate, the more athletic you are likely to be (in the absence of disease). Athletes can have heart rates ranging from 40-60. In others who have heart rates this low due to disease, there are often accompanying symptoms such as dizziness, fainting, feeling unwell which usually require medical attention.

Conversely high pulse rates are also an evidence of ill health and needs further investigation and can be due to endocrine problems like an overactive thyroid. If your pulse rate is high in the absence of disease, regular exercise can help to reduce it by improving the function of your heart but we will discuss exercise later on in this chapter.

Blood sugar

The whole idea of knowing about your blood sugar is to ensure that you are not developing diabetes. Diabetes is a metabolic condition which is basically an inability or reduced ability of your body to handle sugar. The sugar remains in your system and becomes 'toxic' affecting the nerves all over the body resulting in neuropathy. The sugar also affects small blood vessels resulting in damage to small vessels in the kidney (nephropathy), the brain (neuropathy) the heart and essentially all over the body. Uncontrolled diabetes can be a devastating illness but in many people who have developed the illness, it could have been prevented.

> *If you look after your body, your body will look after you.*

There are two main types of diabetes (to look at it simply). Type 1 Diabetes is caused primarily by failure of the insulin producing cells and is usually found in much younger people but of greater importance for our purpose is Type 2 Diabetes which is caused by the body not being able to use the insulin it has, to reduce blood sugar and is generally found in older people. There are strong dietary factors and other associations such as family history with Type 2 Diabetes.

The prevention of Diabetes is important due to the significant health related problems (morbidity) and death (mortality) associated with it especially when it is mostly preventable. In most people who develop Type 2 Diabetes they pass through a phase called Impaired Glucose Tolerance or Pre-Diabetes as referred to by some people. Normal blood sugar is between 3.5 and 6.0mmol/L but in this phase the blood sugar is between 6.1mmol/L and 6.9mmol/L (110-125mg/dL). Lifestyle changes adopted at this stage can still prevent the onset of diabetes which is why monitoring and knowing your numbers can be very useful. Once the blood sugar is repeatedly above 7.0mmol/L (126mg/dL), then a diagnosis of diabetes is made and by this stage it is often irreversible medically speaking.

Blood cholesterol.

This is a measure of the amount of fat in your system and is usually measured by a blood test. Although cholesterol is required in the body for normal functioning, high cholesterol is an independent risk factor for strokes and heart attacks so it is well worth knowing what your level is and managing it accordingly. Cholesterol can be viewed simply as a reading of total cholesterol which is supposed to be less than 5.2mmol/L (200mg/dL) or in its various forms which include LDL cholesterol, HDL cholesterol, triglycerides and more.

To keep it simple, levels of less than 5.2mmol/L (200mg/dL) is associated with low risk of developing heart disease and above this the risks increase. Cholesterol is found in animal fat, cheese, egg yolk, beef, pork, poultry, fish, and shrimp. If your cholesterol is high then adjusting your diet to ensure that less of these foods are eaten will help to bring down your cholesterol and reduce your risk of heart disease.

BMI

This refers to your Body Mass Index and is an index of weight versus height. It is actually calculated by weight in kilograms divided by height in metres squared. The BMI is an indication of whether an individual is underweight (<18), normal (18-24.9), overweight (25-29.9) or obese (>30). At the moment there are lots of scientific discussions as to how accurate it is as it unfairly declares as obese very muscular individuals over those who have a leaner frame for example but it still has its uses as a measure of obesity.

Obesity is now very clearly implicated in various medical conditions such has heart disease, Type 2 diabetes, osteoarthritis, some cancers and obstructive sleep apnoea. Being overweight is unhealthy and sets you on the road to develop many of these conditions and keeping your BMI within the normal range ensures you are doing what you can to prevent some of these conditions. In fact looking through all the indices we have discussed starting from the blood pressure, the pulse, the blood sugar, blood cholesterol and finally BMI the primary initial management boils down to two things you can do for yourself: diet and exercise. In other words I have explained all these indices to say that what you eat and how you use your body matters.

Obesity is now considered one of the major epidemics of the 21st Century and managing it has been considered a

Blood pressure is important in heart attacks and strokes. It is a significant predictor of these illnesses and of sudden death.

priority for many governments. Obesity is naturally managed by a combination of diet and exercise. We will discuss a few things about them and then I will close this chapter.

Diet and Exercise

The word 'diet' sends shivers down the spine of many people. They remember what they promise to do at the beginning of every New Year and how they have failed to lose weight and have to start the process all over again. Diet simply means, 'intake of food'. A good diet does not have to starve you, and there are many diets out there which are useful but any diet that does not recommend a regular exercise plan along with it is probably not doing enough. Diet and exercise must go together to achieve best results.

Our food consists of carbohydrates, proteins and fat along with minerals and vitamins. All food is good when eaten in the right amounts. We should ensure that we eat healthily to keep us effective in our daily life. When you eat too much you become slow, sluggish and your productivity reduces.

In Ecclesiastes 10:17 the Bible says:

Happy is the land whose king is a noble leader and whose leaders feast at the proper time to gain strength for their work, not to get drunk.

In this passage we read that we are to eat for strength and not for drunkenness. In other words, although we are to enjoy our food, the primary reason for eating is for strength and not pleasure. So the foods we eat should strengthen us, not weaken us or clog up our arteries. We should not eat just because we are hungry but because we want to be physically strong. This means we need to pay attention to the health benefits (or lack thereof) of what we eat. It also means we should not eat as a means of relieving stress or pressure and certainly our eating should not be resulting in uncontrollable weight gain.

What should we eat?

Lots of fruit and vegetables as a first rule. Less fried or fatty foods as second, as oily foods will raise your cholesterol. Grill more, fry less. Don't always eat! Fast regularly, not just in January or June when your church or religion declares a fast. Scientists have long studied the beneficial effects of fasting. A study from the University of Illinois in Chicago has done some work showing health benefits from fasting. It helps to cleanse the system and promotes the growth of healthy bacteria which help us develop a strong immune system.

Exercise

I will define exercise as any bodily activity carried out to enhance or maintain fitness, health or wellness. Exercise improves the cardiovascular system, improves the immune system, improves brain function, reduces depression and improves sleep. Twenty minutes of vigorous exercise at least three times weekly is recommended in order to enjoy the health benefits of exercise. It has been proven that the benefits of regular exercise are independent of weight loss. This means if you exercise regularly, in line with our definition of at least 20 minutes of vigorous exercise three times a week, even if you are not losing weight, you will still enjoy many of the benefits attributed to exercising.

Faith Healing

I cannot end this chapter on the Physical Decasection without discussing faith healing. Faith healing is exactly what it says, healing by faith. Faith healing is also known as Divine Healing. Although I am a practicing General Practitioner I believe in faith healing and I practice faith healing. About twenty five years ago I came across certain passages of the Bible that intrigued me. 1 Peter 2:24b says

He personally carried our sins in his body on the cross so that we can be dead to sin and live for what is right. By his wounds you are healed.

Exodus 23:25-26 says

You must serve only the LORD your God. If you do, I will bless you with food and water, and I will protect you from illness. There will be no miscarriages or infertility in your land, and I will give you long, full lives.

Psalm 103:1-5 says

Let all that I am praise the LORD; with my whole heart, I will praise his holy name. Let all that I am praise the LORD; may I never forget the good things he does for me. He forgives all my sins and heals all my diseases. He redeems me from death and crowns me with love and tender mercies. He fills my life with good things. My youth is renewed like the eagle's!

1 John 3:8b says

But the Son of God came to destroy the works of the devil.

The passages above and many other scriptures came alive to me and I realised that healing was an integral part of the salvation package. It is God's will for me to be healthy and well. Looking through the gospels we see Jesus healing people all the time indicating that health and healing is the will of God. Peter said of Jesus in Acts 10:38

> And you know that God anointed Jesus of Nazareth with the Holy Spirit and with power. Then Jesus went around doing good and healing all who were oppressed by the devil, for God was with him.

Jesus healed ALL that were oppressed of the devil. Jesus was passionate about health and wholeness which is why he went about healing people. This means our bodies are important and should be treated with respect. Sickness and disease are oppressions of the devil and Jesus healed ALL that had them. We need to come to that place where we are able to exercise our faith based on the word of God in order to enjoy the healing that God has already provided for us as part of the salvation package.

How then can we practically walk in faith healing? Let me give you my **A** to **G** formula.

1. **A**ccept that God's plan is for you to be healed and whole. You can see that from the scriptural references.

2. **B**elieve in your heart what Jesus has done for us the area of healing. Meditate on the word of God regarding healing till it becomes faith in your heart. You accept with your head but believe with your heart.

3. **C**onfess God's word for healing into your body regularly even when you feel well.

4. **D**ecide to practice faith healing on yourself and others in small areas like minor headaches, mild flu-like illnesses. Pray for yourself using the word of God and expect to be

healed. As your faith develops in small things you will be able to extend it to bigger things.

5. Evaluate your progress, how are things going? Do you need to spend more time meditating on the word of God?

6. Fight for your health and wholeness. Remember the devil will not give up without a battle! Do not be ignorant of his devices.

7. Glorify God by thanking Him in advance for your health and wholeness.

CAUTION!: If you are on medically prescribed medication for conditions like high blood pressure, diabetes or other chronic illnesses, DO NOT stop them suddenly without appropriate professional medical advice. In Luke 5:14, Jesus clearly told a leper to go and show himself to the priests for examination and corroboration of his healing and to offer the relevant sacrifices. He said,

> "Go to the priest and let him examine you. Take along the offering required in the law of Moses for those who have been healed of leprosy. This will be a public testimony that you have been cleansed."

Please DO NOT stop medically prescribed medication unless advised to do so by your doctor. I know people who have been healed of blood pressure. They were on medication for high blood pressure for a while but eventually the blood pressure became very low. The medication was reduced and eventually we had to stop it. That is how it should be done, not independently and not without medical advice.

RIGHT QUESTIONS, RIGHT ANSWERS

1. Why is this Decasection important?

Your body is your passport to function on this earth. You need to know all your numbers and work on them. (BP, BMI, Blood Glucose, Blood cholesterol). They are independent risk factors for strokes, heart attacks and other chronic conditions. Keeping them under control significantly reduces the likelihood of having either of those conditions.

2. What must you do to invest in this Decasection of your life? Whatever you do not invest in will depreciate and deteriorate.

You should make healthy eating and regular exercise a standard in your life. In addition to that, regular checks with your doctor and depending on your age, regular blood tests to ensure you are effectively managing your numbers. You should also seek to develop your capacity to practice faith healing and live a life of health, strength and wholeness.

DECASECTION

Five

MENTAL

The word 'mental' refers to the realm of your soul. In order to understand this properly, let us first of all establish the fact that man is made up of spirit, soul and body. 1 Thessalonians 5:23 says

> Now may the God of peace make you holy in every way, and may your whole spirit and soul and body be kept blameless until our Lord Jesus Christ comes again.

In Ephesians 3:20 you will read

> Now all glory to God, who is able, through his mighty power at work within us, to accomplish infinitely more than we might ask or think.

The Bible refers to the phrase 'may your whole...', which suggests that we are incomplete without our whole spirit, soul and body. With our spirits we relate with God and the realm of the spirit, with our bodies we relate with the natural realm but with our souls we relate with the intellectual, emotional and psychological realms.

The Bible sometimes uses the word 'heart' instead of 'soul'

or 'mind'. In Proverbs 4:23 it says 'Guard your heart above all else, for it determines the course of your life.' The state of your heart or soul will determine the course of your life. The state of your heart will determine the things you say or do. This is how Luke 6:45 puts it.

A good person produces good things from the treasury of a good heart, and an evil person produces evil things from the treasury of an evil heart. What you say flows from what is in your heart.

Good things come from a good heart and evil things come from an evil heart. So it is imperative that we ensure our hearts are good and not evil as the outcome of our lives depends on it. The Bible also says in 2 Timothy 1:7

For God has not given us a spirit of fear and timidity, but of power, love and of self-discipline.

To function effectively you need a sound mind that can handle the pressures of life. There are three main aspects to you mentally; your mind, your emotions and your will. Your mind is the part of you that thinks, your emotions are the part of you that feels, and your will is the part of you that decides. Let us look at each one in turn.

The Mind

The mind can be defined as the seat of thought and memory, ideas and perceptions, reasoning and concentration. Your mind is the part of you that thinks. Thoughts come from your mind. In other words your mind generates and stores thoughts. Your mind is the window to your soul. Everything that goes into your soul has to pass through your mind. Most of the battles of life are fought and won in the mind. Henry Ford once said 'if you think you can, you can, and if you think you can't you're right'.

Your thoughts refer to the images projected by your mind. It is well known that your life will flow in the direction of your strongest thoughts. That's why the Bible says in Proverbs 23:7 from the New King James Version 'As he thinks in his heart so is he'. Even when a person's words say different, his true self is determined by how he thinks and what he thinks.

Earlier on we mentioned that your mind generates and stores thoughts. It is therefore important that you train your mind to generate and store good, productive and wholesome thoughts so that your life can produce good, productive and wholesome fruit. The key thing to remember is that your mind is like a computer. It will give you back what you have put in it. If you feed your mind with wholesome material it will think wholesome thoughts but if you feed your mind with defiling material you will end up with defiling thoughts. The process of feeding your mind, we can also refer to as education. Now apart from formal education, you can informally educate your mind with information that will benefit you. For example by reading this book you are educating yourself in the understanding of the Decasections. This education will allow you to generate thoughts about what you should and should not do and those thoughts when they have taken root, will become knowledge or information stored as memories, resulting in altered behaviour.

In order to grow spiritually you must educate your mind with the word of God. Romans 12:2 and James 1:21 say

Don't copy the behavior and customs of this world, but let God transform you into a new person by changing the way you think. Then you will learn to know God's will for you, which is good and pleasing and perfect.

So get rid of all the filth and evil in your lives, and humbly accept the word God has planted in your hearts, for it has the power to save your souls.

Spiritual growth comes by feeding your mind with the word of God. Mental development will help you professionally, will help you influence society and will help you make good decisions.

Professional Development

Any form of growth comes from feeding the mind. In order to grow professionally, you have to feed your mind with up to date information about your profession. Paul advised Timothy to maintain his professional credibility and standing by studying; in other words feeding his mind with knowledge. 2 Timothy 2:15 from the King James Version says

Study to shew thyself approved unto God, a workman that needeth not to be ashamed, rightly dividing the word of truth.

This is very important as many people are either not in the careers they want to be in or are operating far below their capabilities due to a lack of development in this area of the soul. Paul said to Timothy, "STUDY; develop yourself in the job that you are doing and you will be a workman that does not need to be ashamed." Likewise if we study or develop ourselves mentally in our businesses, careers, profession or academic endeavour we will generally be one of the best at what we do and we will have no need to be ashamed.

Age is no barrier to education. What may have been pioneering information yesterday when you first studied is probably obsolete today. Dr Mensah Otabil, a clergy man from Ghana, gave an analogy many years ago. Take a man or woman about 30 years of age with no university degree. If he or she starts a university course, they would be done in three or four years for most courses. Embarking on a Master's degree will see completion by about the age of 35-36. If a PhD programme is to be started, by about the age of 40 the person could have a doctorate. Now the interesting thing is this: if you do nothing those 10 years will pass anyway, but if you choose to engage in mental development you can be 40 with a PhD rather than 40 without one.

Now it's not just about getting a university education or having a PhD, it's about developing yourself mentally to enhance what you do. A former pastor of mine told us some years back that he attended a course on public speaking. Everyone was wondering 'why' as he was one of the most prolific communicators you would ever have sat under. The pastor explained that no matter how good you are at something always seek to improve, always seek to learn, always seek to better yourself, in other words seek to develop yourself mentally. Mental development will aid your professional development.

Influencing society

If you want to influence society, if God will use you to bring about significant policy or political change in this day and age, it is a major advantage to be an intellectual; and this comes by mental development. Now before you say you are not interested remember there are people sitting in high places called 'think-tanks' who determine the policy of this nation. One of the most recent to affect us in the United Kingdom, as at the time of writing, is the re-definition of marriage. God needs His people to infiltrate these areas and make a difference.

Being an intellectual positions you in places where your light can shine brighter for Jesus. Jesus infiltrated the religious culture of His day. Was He an intellectual? Yes. The Pharisees said about Him: How come this guy knows letters having never learned? Daniel and his friends found their way into high political office because they were intellectuals.

Then the king ordered Ashpenaz, his chief of staff, to bring to the palace some of the young men of Judah's royal family and other noble families, who had been brought to Babylon as captives. "Select only strong, healthy, and good-looking young men," he said. "Make sure they are well versed in every branch of learning, are gifted with knowledge and good judgment, and are suited to serve in the royal palace. Train these young men in the language and literature of Babylon.

Daniel 1:3-4

God gave these four young men an unusual aptitude for understanding every aspect of literature and wisdom. And God gave Daniel the special ability to interpret the meanings of visions and dreams.

When the training period ordered by the king was completed, the chief of staff brought all the young men to

King Nebuchadnezzar. The king talked with them, and no one impressed him as much as Daniel, Hananiah, Mishael, and Azariah. So they entered the royal service. Whenever the king consulted them in any matter requiring wisdom and balanced judgment, he found them ten times more capable than any of the magicians and enchanters in his entire kingdom. *(Daniel 1:17-20)*

Decision making.

Decisions are made through the complex process of acquisition of information which we call knowledge, assimilation of information which we call understanding and application of information which we call wisdom. Jesus encourages us to be systematic in our decision making.

> But don't begin until you count the cost. For who would begin construction of a building without first calculating the cost to see if there is enough money to finish it? Otherwise, you might complete only the foundation before running out of money, and then everyone would laugh at you. They would say, 'There's the person who started that building and couldn't afford to finish it!' "Or what king would go to war against another king without first sitting down with his counselors to discuss whether his army of 10,000 could defeat the 20,000 soldiers marching against him? And if he can't, he will send a delegation to discuss terms of peace while the enemy is still far away. *(Luke 14:28-32)*

Jesus in the passage above is talking about being rational, sensible and not emotional in your decision making. He is saying don't be carried away with making emotional decisions, let your thinking be clear when making difficult life choices especially those that will potentially cost you something. Jesus said 'count the cost' which means be aware of all possible factors. The New King James version of the bible uses the phrase 'sit down first and consider' which means conduct an assessment: is this going to be a profitable venture or not? Mental

> *To function effectively you need a sound mind that can handle the pressures of life.*

development will help your decision making by ensuring you are aware of all the variables when dealing with a situation.

How can we pursue mental development?

1.   Pray to God to give you wisdom, James 1:5 says

'If any of you lacks wisdom, let him ask of God, who gives to all liberally and without reproach, and it will be given to him.'

God gave Daniel wisdom and skill in all learning. Ask God to bless your mind and intellect.

2.   Read books-spiritual books, professional books, study a course that will position you better in your career or even allow you to change career if you want to, educate yourself online or through tuition. It has been said that if you spend 20 minutes on a topic every day, you will become an expert within a short space of time.

3.   Read about your situation, acquire information, assimilate the information you acquire, apply the information you have assimilated. The choices and decisions you made yesterday have determined the life you live now and the

choices and decisions you make today will determine the life you will live tomorrow.

Emotional Stability

The mind is the part of you that thinks. Likewise your emotions are the part of you that feel. There are a very wide range of emotions which can sometimes be combined to form even more complex emotions but based on work done over the years, psychologists have identified 6 basic emotions: Happy, Exited, Tender, Scared, Angry and Sad. The interesting thing about emotions is that they are based on what is happening around you. Your emotions are your response to the various environmental stimuli you are exposed to. For example if you are exposed to something pleasurable, you feel happy, maybe even exited. If however you are exposed to something less pleasurable you may feel sadness or anger or you may even be scared depending on what external stimulus you are exposed to.

Your emotional response to a particular situation is largely dependent on your personality type. Tim La Haye an author and Christian minister wrote an excellent book called 'Spirit controlled temperament' which highlights the effect our personality type has on our moods, decisions and behaviour. His book highlights the importance of understanding your personality but then allowing the Holy Spirit to mould you and make you a better person. What is however most important for me is the fact that your emotions are supposed to be subject to your spirit or to your person. 2 Timothy 1:7 states

For God has not given us a spirit of fear and timidity, but of power, love, and self-discipline.

So you can see that self-discipline, self-control and self-mastery is the real focus. You can find yourself in a situation that makes you very angry but if expressing your anger will be unproductive then self-discipline will find more productive ways of expressing your concerns rather than exploding (or imploding!) 1 Corinthians 9:27 says

I discipline my body like an athlete, training it to do what it should. Otherwise, I fear that after preaching to others I myself might be disqualified.

We need to discipline ourselves to respond appropriately to situations rather than inflame them. Ephesians 4:26-32

And "don't sin by letting anger control you." Don't let the sun go down while you are still angry, for anger gives a foothold to the devil. If you are a thief, quit stealing. Instead, use your hands for good hard work, and then give generously to others in need. Don't use foul or abusive language. Let everything you say be good and helpful, so that your words will be an encouragement to those who hear them. And do not bring sorrow to God's Holy Spirit by the way you live. Remember, he has identified you as his own, guaranteeing that you will be saved on the day of redemption. Get rid of all bitterness, rage, anger, harsh words, and slander, as well as all types of evil behaviour. Instead, be kind to each other, tender-hearted, forgiving one another, just as God through Christ has forgiven you.

From this passage you can see that the overall message here is do not let negative emotions get the better of you but control yourself to express positive emotions only. The build up of negative emotions results in one of the greatest maladies of the 20th and 21st centuries a widespread phenomenon called 'Depression'.

Depression results when the build up of negative emotion in you overwhelms you and starts to determine your life, your actions, your behaviour and your decision making. It is characterised by low mood, poor motivation, poor sleep, feeling anxious and stressed and in many people it is connected to an incident or incidents that have occurred in their past. The worst thing about depression is that it is contagious. Depressed people depress people.

> Work at living in peace with everyone, and work at living a holy life, for those who are not holy will not see the Lord. Look after each other so that none of you fails to receive the grace of God. Watch out that no poisonous root of bitterness grows up to trouble you, corrupting many. *(Hebrews 12:14-15)*

From this passage we not only see that bitterness or depression is contagious we see that the solution is to work at living in peace with everyone. In fact it is so contagious that we are encouraged to look out for each other to ensure we are not infected.

Depression may lead to alcoholism, drug abuse and illicit sexual acts as people look for artificial highs to mask the lows inside them. Some people turn to violence and vandalism in a bid to hurt someone else so that others can feel their pain. It all starts with the build up of negative emotion inside us.

Please don't get me wrong, many people have been terribly

hurt through child abuse, sexual abuse, physical or emotional abuse. These people have been hurt deeply as a result of what they have suffered and if the cycle of hurt and pain is not broken, it will lead to mental illness, and some have suffered severe mental breakdowns due to their inability to cope.

Living in peace with everyone cannot be overstated. If we are rash with our words we may hurt people (see Ephesians 4:29 above) and this could also start its own cycle of hurt and negative emotions which is why Jesus said we will have to account for every idle word we have spoken. Matthew 12:35-37 says

> A good person produces good things from the treasury of a good heart, and an evil person produces evil things from the treasury of an evil heart. And I tell you this, you must give an account on judgment day for every idle word you speak. The words you say will either acquit you or condemn you.

How can we deal with depression and mental illness? It depends on how severe it is. Talking therapy is the first line of treatment; and this includes counselling, Cognitive Behavioural Therapy (CBT) which simply means re-configuring your thinking. Romans 12:2 supports CBT:

> Don't copy the behavior and customs of this world, but let God transform you into a new person by changing the way you think. Then you will learn to know God's will for you, which is good and pleasing and perfect.

This transformation of your thinking (which is essentially what CBT does) is available spiritually through personal reading of the word of God or through your local church in the form of Bible study, listening to sermons and speaking to pastors and leaders. It is also available medically through various counselling organisations. If depression is very severe you may be required to see a psychiatrist who will probably recommend medication to help you through the difficult phase and you can then be weaned off medication eventually. I must stress though, that a lot of this can be

> *Your emotional response to a particular situation is largely dependent on your personality type.*

avoided by preventing the build-up of negative emotions in you.

The will

We defined your mind as the part of you that thinks, your emotions as the part of you that feels and your will as the part of you that decides. We have already mentioned decision making earlier on which is improved by mental development but we want to look at the will as a concept on its own.

Your will is the arbitrator of yourself. It is influenced by both your spiritual and your natural inclinations. What you do is dependent on 'who' is the overriding force at every point in time. If your natural inclinations are strong then you will do predominantly natural things and if your spiritual inclinations are strong you will do predominantly spiritual things. In every situation you find yourself; there is a best possible option in the mind of God.

That is what the Scriptures mean when they say, "No eye has seen, no ear has heard, and no mind has imagined what

God has prepared for those who love him." But it was to us that God revealed these things by his Spirit. For his Spirit searches out everything and shows us God's deep secrets. *(1 Corinthians 2:9-10)*

> But people who aren't spiritual can't receive these truths from God's Spirit. It all sounds foolish to them and they can't understand it, for only those who are spiritual can understand what the Spirit means. Those who are spiritual can evaluate all things, but they themselves cannot be evaluated by others. *(1 Corinthians 2:14-15)*

> Don't copy the behaviour and customs of this world, but let God transform you into a new person by changing the way you think. Then you will learn to know God's will for you, which is good and pleasing and perfect. *(Romans 12:2)*

Certain things are clear from the verses above: God has a preferred outcome for every situation. If you are not spiritual you are not likely to take decisions based on the Spirit of God. However if you allow God's word to transform your mind you will learn to know God's will for you which you can then act on.

Making decisions is an integral part of life. You wake up in the morning and have to decide what to eat, what to wear, where to go and what to do. With time, certain decisions become easier based on certain behaviour patterns you have developed, good or bad. From the beginning of time man has always been faced with choices. In the Garden of Eden, Adam had to choose between eating the forbidden fruit and not eating. In Genesis 12, Abraham had to choose between staying in Ur of the Chaldees and moving to Canaan. In the days of Elijah, he placed a choice before the children of Israel either to serve God or serve Baal. There can be no sitting on the fence.

Someone once said 'We can try to avoid making decisions by doing nothing, but even that is a decision'. Jesus Himself had a choice to make when pondering the cross in the garden of Gethsemane. After Jesus died, Peter had to make a choice between returning to life as a fisherman and being used of God in the propagation of the gospel. There is nothing new under the sun, in the journey of life we will all have to make certain choices.

The quality of the decisions we make will determine the outcome of our lives

Any decision we take or do not take will affect our lives in one way or another. I like the way a lady called Flora Whittemore put it, she said: 'The doors we open and close each day decide the lives we live.' Who to be, who to hang out with, who to listen to, who to marry, if to marry, what to do in life, what to study, what to believe, if to believe.

In Deuteronomy 30:15, Moses made it unambiguously clear that we can determine the outcome of our lives by the choices we make and the decisions we take.

> Now listen! Today I am giving you a choice between life and death, between prosperity and disaster.

How can I ensure that my decisions are good ones? James 3:13-18 has what I call the check list of wisdom:

> If you are wise and understand God's ways, prove it by living

an honorable life, doing good works with the humility that comes from wisdom. But if you are bitterly jealous and there is selfish ambition in your heart, don't cover up the truth with boasting and lying. For jealousy and selfishness are not God's kinds of wisdom. Such things are earthly, unspiritual, and demonic. For wherever there is jealousy and selfish ambition, there you will find disorder and evil of every kind. But the wisdom from above is first of all pure. It is also peace loving, gentle at all times, and willing to yield to others. It is full of mercy and good deeds. It shows no favoritism and is always sincere. And those who are peacemakers will plant seeds of peace and reap a harvest of righteousness.

If you are taking a decision that will glorify God certain things must be evident about the decision:

1. It must lead to you doing good works.

2. It must reflect humility.

3. It must not be a function of jealousy.

4. There must be no selfish ambition.

5. It must reflect purity.

6. It must be peace loving.

7. It must be gentle and willing to yield to God (and godly leadership).

8. It must be full of mercy.

9. It must be free from favouritism.

10. It must plant seeds of peace and reap a harvest of righteousness.

So how can I apply this to significant decisions like taking a job or marrying a spouse? Suppose I am offered a job and I have prayed and feel strongly that this is the job for me. I then ask these ten questions. Will I be doing good? Am I being humble? Am I trying to outdo someone else? If the Lord or a godly spiritual leader says no, will I be willing to listen? Do I have peace in my heart as a result of my decision or do I feel unsettled?

Likewise with respect to marriage, why do I feel this is the person the Lord has for me? Why do I even want to marry? Am I pursuing selfish ambition or do I see God's purpose in it? Am I willing to let go if God or a spiritual mentor says so? Am I emotionally involved (favouritism) or am I spiritually open to God on this matter? Am I lusting or am I in purity? Am I being sincere in my answers?

Once you have employed the checklist and you feel satisfied that you have ensured that you are in the will of God then go ahead and take the decision. God will honour you with peace and your decision will produce a harvest of righteousness which means many people will be blessed by your decision.

RIGHT QUESTIONS, RIGHT ANSWERS

1. Why is this Decasection important?

This decasection is important because feeding or rightly educating your mind will result in professional development, rightly influencing society and taking right decisions. We must at all costs avoid a build up of negative emotion to avoid depression and other mental illness. We are responsible for the lives we live based on the decisions we have and have not taken.

2. What must you do to invest in this Decasection of your life? Whatever you donot invest in will depreciate and deteriorate.

Essentially ensuring you are reading, studying, improving yourself mentally, freeing yourself of negative emotions and acknowledging God in all your decisions (including the mundane ones) would be a good place to start.

DECASECTION

Six

MARITAL

This refers to your marriage. It involves the whole process of deciding whether to marry, deciding to marry, finding a spouse, getting married and having a happy fulfilling marriage. We won't be able to cover everything in detail but one day I may write a book on marriage.

Very many books have been written on the subject of marriage and capturing all of this in one chapter will be very difficult but let's look at marriage from a slightly different point of view. I will address this area under three headings- Why should I marry, Who should I marry and How can I have a happy marriage.

Why Should I marry?

The primary reason for marriage is to fulfil purpose. God said in Genesis 2:18

> Then the Lord God said, "It is not good for the man to be alone. I will make a helper who is just right for him.

Other words for helper are collaborator, partner, aide, assistant. We are to help each other, collaborate with each other, partner each other, aid each other, and assist each other in fulfilling purpose. Your marriage has a purpose. While we were courting, Dami and I had a day of the week set aside for fasting and prayer. On one of the days as we prayed, we felt the Lord telling us that our marriage was going to be a beacon of light for Him to the world. So we have comported ourselves with that purpose in mind: God wants to use our marriage to glorify Him. When the purpose of a thing is not known, abuse is inevitable. Discovering the purpose of your marriage will help secure it and anchor it to God.

The secondary reason for marriage is companionship. The Bible says in Ecclesiastes 4:7-12

> I observed yet another example of something meaningless under the sun. This is the case of a man who is all alone, without a child or a brother, yet who works hard to gain as much wealth as he can. But then he asks himself, "Who am I working for? Why am I giving up so much pleasure now?" It is all so meaningless and depressing. Two people are better off than one, for they can help each other succeed. If one person falls, the other can reach out and help. But someone who falls alone is in real trouble. Likewise, two people lying close together can keep each other warm. But how can one be warm alone? A person standing alone can be attacked and defeated, but two can stand back-to-back and conquer. Three are even better, for a triple-braided cord is not easily broken.

Loneliness causes depression and selfishness. Loneliness makes us weak. No man is an island it is often said. No one is designed to be alone. Man was designed to live in a community and that starts with a family preceded by a relationship. God clearly said that it is not good for man to be alone. That means it is good to have a companion.

From the passage we see above we can conclude on a few things.

- Life is meaningless and depressing if faced alone
- Life is easier when you have someone to help
- Life's falls are cushioned by the presence of a companion
- Life can be conquered when in partnership

This makes me conclude that life is sweeter when shared with someone you love. Life is more fulfilling when approached with someone you care about. Life takes on new meaning and new focus when you are sharing it. Facing your purpose is more fruitful when engaged in it with a companion. Dami is my best friend, my confidant, my counsellor. We spend time together, we can discuss anything and I seek her advice on everything just like I would with a best friend. Her opinion matters to me; we are genuinely friends.

> *The primary reason for marriage is to fulfil purpose.*

For me, the third reason for marriage would be sexual fulfilment. Scientists tell us the sex drive is second only to the survival instinct. Unfortunately many people of Christian faith down play this element of life to their detriment. If you look at society today we see everything being sexualised; toys, sweets, car adverts and even loans! As a result, the sexual pressures we find ourselves exposed to are immense. Marriage provides a legitimate avenue for sexual fulfilment. Hebrews 13:4 says

> Give honour to marriage, and remain faithful to one another
> in marriage. God will surely judge people who are immoral
> and those who commit adultery.

The Bible says marriage is honourable. With many people leaving marriage until much later or not marrying at all, a lot of people are getting involved in sexual practices which unfortunately lead to sexual problems when they do marry, resulting in extra-marital affairs, addiction to pornography and other sexual vices. With so much focus on the career in this day and age, many people are not getting married until their 30s and our sexual drives are highest in our late teens and twenties. This begs the question, how do these people cope with their sexual urges and drives? The answer is they do not! Studies have shown that married couples are more sexually fulfilled than their unmarried counterparts.

The fourth reason for marriage would be procreation (having children). God gave a command in Genesis 1:28:

> Then God blessed them and said, "Be fruitful and multiply.
> Fill the earth and govern it. Reign over the fish in the sea,
> the birds in the sky, and all the animals that scurry along the
> ground."

We have been commanded to be fruitful and multiply. Psalm 127:3 also says

> Children are a gift from the LORD; they are a reward from
> him.

Children are a blessing, a gift from God. Children born into a stable family with both parents present are more likely to grow up responsible. We discuss this in more detail in the Family Decasection. It is also worth mentioning that marriage has health benefits. Although this in itself is not a reason to get married, research has shown that those who are married are healthier and live longer than those who are not.

Who should I marry?

This question is the meat of the matter or bone of contention when it comes to marriage. Is there just one person out there for me or can I choose from a range of people? Does it really matter who I marry? These are the questions a lot of unmarried people ask. My response is this: If we really believe that our lives are in God's hands; if we really believe that God knows what is best for us; if we really believe that God knows our future, then in His wisdom, He will know who best fits the bill for our lives.

Remember one of the qualities of a true worshiper is walking in the Spirit. I believe that God has an ideal life He would like us to live. I have made this clear in the chapter on Purpose. We have a marking scheme for our lives. This ideal life includes what we should be doing but also who we should be doing it with.

Psalm 139:16 says

You saw me before I was born. Every day of my life was recorded in your book. Every moment was laid out before a single day had passed.

So I believe God has a preferred choice for us and He is more than able to direct us to His preferred choice as we walk in the Spirit. Romans 8:14 says

For all who are led by the Spirit of God are children of God.

We should allow God to lead and direct us to His choice for us. The modern concept of serial dating until you find someone you think you can make it work with is damaging and leaves a lot of young people broken hearted. I believe in having friendships with members of the opposite sex, but once you start identifying someone from the crowd as a special person, then you should start asking for God's direction before you get too emotionally involved. At that point, getting clarity is difficult due to your clouded emotions.

However in considering potential spouses there are certain pointers to be aware of. The person you should marry will have certain primary characteristics. If these primary characteristics are not there then you should make it clear that you are simply friends and marriage is not on the cards to avoid raising and then dashing hopes.

These are the primary characteristics to look out for:

1. The person must be designed to support you and help you in fulfilling your purpose. This is a spiritual quality.

It goes without saying that if purpose is the most important thing in life then the spouse that God will have for us will be someone who will help us fulfil purpose. This means that the person must share your spiritual beliefs and values and you should have complementary visions and purposes in life as support works both ways. If you are considering getting married and your spouse has no concept of purpose or vision, and no focus or direction in life then beware. This obviously means you should have a concept of your purpose and vision

90

in life and the chapter on purpose would help you start to develop that.

When I was in secondary school my plan was to marry a teacher who would have time to care for our children. I grew up with a strong sense of family and I felt at the time that teachers, by reason of their working hours would make the best wives and mothers. This would mean if I was out working, my wife would be available for the children. (My mother was a teacher so I guess there was some family influence there!) I didn't marry a teacher but I married a nurse whose overriding desire in life was to be a homemaker (good wife and mother). This complemented my desire to be out there being a blessing to people either through my profession or through my church involvement. In that way we support each other to fulfil our respective purpose, mine to the world at large and hers to the family. However as we are a team, she supports me in reaching the world and covers the areas I cannot. Likewise I support her on the home front; I am very involved with the children and provide for the house. You will have your own core spiritual values which are of prime importance to your sense of family. If these are missing then the foundation is already faulty.

2. The person must be your friend as you will be spending a lot of time together and you need to be able to get on. This is a soul based quality.

You must enjoy each other's company and find pleasure and comfort being together even if you are not doing anything specific. If you consider the fact that you will be spending the rest of your life with this person which could well be up to 70 years or more, you had better be friends! There is this modern concept I have heard about not being able to marry your friend. You will often hear ladies say, 'I can't marry him, he is my best friend'. That's probably exactly who you should marry! The fantasy of a Prince Charming or a Princess Bella who gets all your romantic juices going is a fairy tale. Will you still like this person in a few years when baldness sets in, when you realise their hair is not real or when they look very different without make up? Things like that do not bother you about your friend and they should not bother you about your spouse. You should enjoy the personality and company of your spouse to be.

3. The person must be someone you are physically attracted to as you will eventually have to be sexually fulfilled by this person when you get married. This is a physical quality.

If you look at the other primary qualities above; the first one is spiritual and is the most important. The second one is of the soul and comes next. The third one is the body which completes the whole man (spirit, soul and body). However let us be aware that what attracts us differs. I am beginning to understand that what makes us 'sexy' has more to do with our personalities than our male and female 'appendages'. How we dress, how we care for ourselves and how we comport ourselves has more to do with how 'sexy' we are perceived to be than our genitals.

The traditional skinny hour-glass woman is not considered sexy in many cultures; and although such women may attract a lot of media attention, many men would rather have normal women. Many women who may be considered overweight are very attractive sexually to their spouses. Likewise some women find bald men very attractive as they are perceived to be very virile and having lots of testosterone. The point is we are different and our views of attractiveness are different. We will find ourselves being attracted to certain types of people and this acts as a pointer to the kind of people we are drawn to or find attractive.

The secondary characteristics of the person you should marry are as varied as there are people, but these include wanting people to come from certain cultures, spouses who can cook or clean, sharing certain hobbies and the list is endless. I won't go into details as that is beyond the remit of this book but if there is anything you must take away from this section, it is that you need to allow God to lead and direct you in choosing a spouse.

My favourite analogy is this: a woman has three potential suitors asking for her hand in marriage. They all seem to fulfil her spirit, soul and body criteria. One will leave her in five years, another will never leave her but will have affairs and the third will love her forever. How does she know the difference today, here and now? A man has three women he is looking at. They all seem to fulfil the spirit, soul and body criteria. One will leave him for a richer man in five years, one will not leave him but will have inappropriate relationships and one will love him and be his soul mate forever. How does he know the difference today, here and now? Only the leading and direction of the One who sees tomorrow will make the difference. This is one of the most important areas of your life in which to seek the guidance of the Holy Spirit.

What should I do to start preparing for a life of marriage?

Once we have taken on board all we have described above, then the preparation for a relationship becomes clear and can be expressed in a few statements.

- Have a purpose in life.

- Be prayerful and learn to walk in the Spirit and understand how the Lord leads and directs you.

- Be a friendly person.

- Look after yourself physically (the way you dress, your appearance and comportment).

How can I have a happy marriage?

Please read this passage from Ephesians 5:21-33 which holds the secret to a happy marriage.

And further, submit to one another out of reverence for Christ. For wives, this means submit to your husbands as to the Lord. For a husband is the head of his wife as Christ is the head of the church. He is the Saviour of his body, the church. As the church submits to Christ, so you wives should submit to your husbands in everything. For husbands, this means love your wives, just as Christ loved the church. He gave up his life for her to make her holy and clean, washed by the cleansing of God's word. He did this to present her to himself as a glorious church without a spot or wrinkle or any other blemish. Instead, she will be holy and without fault. In the same way, husbands ought to love their wives as they love their own bodies. For a man who loves his wife actually shows love for himself. No one hates his own body but feeds and cares for it, just as Christ cares for the church. And we are members of his body. As the Scriptures say, "A man leaves his father and mother and is joined to his wife, and the two are united into one." This is a great mystery, but it is an illustration of the way Christ and the church are one. So again I say, each man must love his wife as he loves himself, and the wife must respect her husband.

The first secret to a happy marriage is submission. Both husband and wife must learn to submit to each other. The wife expresses submission by respecting her husband as the God ordained head of the team, not because he is better or higher but because that is his role. The husband expresses submission by loving his wife. Did you notice the bit about Christ giving His life for the Church? That is how much men are to love their wives. If every man expressed submission by loving his wife and every wife expressed submission by respecting her husband we would have happier marriages.

Women are more prone to disrespect due to their sharp tongues while men are more prone to losing interest due to their wandering eyes, so the instructions from God are very gender specific based on what He knows about us. The beauty of it all is that portion which talks about husband and wife becoming one. As the wife expresses submission by respecting and the husband expresses submission by loving, both husband and wife become more and more one. This reveals to us the goal of marriage.

The goal of marriage is oneness. Until you are becoming more and more one, until you progress more and more into a harmonious state, there will be strife and strain. You are to become so entwined with your spouse that your responses, thoughts and viewpoints about life start to harmonise and become one.

The second secret to a happy marriage is the ability to work through conflict when it arises. As a couple, you must have an agreed manner of dealing with conflict. A good marriage preparation programme will deal with this but allow me to state here that there will be conflict in every relationship as a result of your different personalities, backgrounds, preferences, viewpoints and desires; all of these will potentially cause conflict. However if you remember to submit to each other and work for the good of the marriage rather than the individual then you are more likely to satisfactorily resolve conflicts. It can also be very helpful to have a more experienced couple that both of you trust and respect, to have as mentors to guide you through difficult patches.

The third secret to a happy marriage is to work towards being in agreement in everything you do. Amos 3:3 says

Can two people walk together without agreeing on the direction?

You cannot be in a marriage relationship and not walk in agreement. Marriage is about oneness, which means coming to a place of harmony. Dami and I usually advise young couples to work towards agreeing on as many things as possible, in as many areas of life as possible. We made a pact early in our marriage never to take any major decisions without agreeing. If we cannot agree, we do not take the decision. This makes us discuss everything and the result is that we prioritise our marriage relationship over our individual desires.

The No-Go areas of marriage

There are certain areas of marriage which I refer to as 'no-go' areas. Books on marriage will go into more detail but here are a few:

- Avoid spiritual conflict
- Avoid di-vision (very different purposes in life)
- Avoid undue sexual tensions
- Avoid financial independence
- Avoid unresolved conflict
- Avoid long distance relationships
- Avoid extended family interference

The problems of marital failure

No one wins when a marriage fails. In fact everyone loses. Everyone suffers, everyone feels pain and everyone ends up being damaged. Harsh words but true words. The couple suffers, their children suffer, the family members suffer. I have seen an entire community suffer due to the marital failure of a prominent member of that community. The ripple effect is devastating. Seeds of bitterness are sown, people are hurt and the children grow up affected.

Marital failure must be avoided. If you are yet to marry, make up your mind to make your marriage work. This means, you must ensure you go into marriage with the right frame of mind and the direction of the Lord. Don't end up as a statistic (almost 50 per cent of all marriages end in divorce and the rates in the Church are almost as bad as the rates outside the church).

I was nineteen or twenty when I made up my mind to be the best husband in the world. I made up my mind to make my marriage work, to put in the required

> *Both husband and wife must learn to submit to each other.*

effort and I am grateful to God for the blessing in marriage I am enjoying today. Dami also prayed similar prayers when she was younger. She wanted to be a good wife; in fact she started attending marriage seminars from the age of twelve! Over the years I have discovered that my wife is the most wonderful woman in the whole world. I could not have been blessed by a better person to be my friend, companion, lover and wife. There have been the usual challenges that every marriage goes through but at every point we keep going back to the basic principles and reaffirming to each other that we are in this for the long haul. We always agree to find solutions to whatever challenges we face at whatever cost and God has been extremely faithful.

The devastation caused by marital failure almost makes it better not to marry than to marry and have problems, but the infinite joys and pleasures of a beautiful marriage make it almost inconceivable not to want such a blessing ordained by God.

RIGHT QUESTIONS, RIGHT ANSWERS

1. Why is this Decasection important?

This Decasection is important as who you marry is probably one of the most important decisions you will make in life after the decision to become a Bible believing Christian and living for God. It is important you get it right and for those of us who are already married it is important you make it right.

2. What must you do to invest in this Decasection of your life? Whatever you do not invest in will depreciate and deteriorate.

This is achieved by spending quality time together, regularly reviewing your marriage together on a monthly, quarterly and annual basis and reading books on marriage. Attending couple enrichment programmes or marriage preparation programmes, if you are not yet married, can also be very beneficial.

DECASECTION

Seven

MATERIAL

This chapter will deal with material possessions and what our attitude to them should be and also look at our relationship with material things. I want to start by establishing the fact that God wants us to be blessed and prosperous. In 3 John 2 the New King James Version of the Bible says

> Beloved, I pray that you may prosper in all things and be in health, just as your soul prospers.

God wants us to prosper. It is His plan for us to prosper and be wealthy. God will not desire for us something He has put beyond our reach. If He desires we should prosper then we can be sure He has made provision for us to prosper. According to Psalm 34:10 the Bible says:

> Even strong young lions sometimes go hungry, but those who trust in the LORD will lack no good thing.

God does not want us to lack any of the good things of life, whether they be nice houses or good cars. In 1 Timothy 6:17b the Bible says

> 'Their trust should be in God, who richly gives us all we

need for our enjoyment.'

All we need for our enjoyment! That sounds like the good life to me! 2 Peter 1:3a also says

'By his divine power, God has given us everything we need for living a godly life.'

God has given us everything we need to live a godly life. A godly life is one that is lived like God. God does not live in poverty; His streets are made of gold. God lives in abundance and He has declared that everything we need is provided for us in advance. Everything we need to make it in life has been given to us already. Glory to God! This is how Deuteronomy 8:18 puts it:

Remember the LORD your God. He is the one who gives you power to be successful, in order to fulfil the covenant he confirmed to your ancestors with an oath.

Also in 2 Corinthians 8:9 the Bible says

You know the generous grace of our Lord Jesus Christ. Though he was rich, yet for your sakes he became poor, so that by his poverty he could make you rich.

We cannot escape it, we cannot explain it away. God wants us to be rich; He wants us to be wealthy. The life of Abraham, Isaac and Jacob, the founding fathers of faith are a further clear example. When we look at their lives with all the challenges they had, it is clear that there is something they did not lack, wealth. In Genesis 26:12-14 the Bible says

When Isaac planted his crops that year, he harvested a hundred times more grain than he planted, for the LORD blessed him. He became a very rich man, and his wealth continued to grow. He acquired so many flocks of sheep and goats, herds of cattle, and servants that the Philistines became jealous of him.

In verse 12 the Bible says God blessed Isaac but in verse 13 the Bible goes on to say that Isaac became a very rich man and his wealth continued to grow meaning he got richer and richer. We could go on and on giving examples of Solomon or even Jabez, who started out in life as an average Joe but he prayed for his circumstances to change and God honoured him (1 Chronicles 4:9-10).

What is clear is that God's plan for us is to be blessed with material wealth. However it is extremely important that with the same fervour with which I have established that God wants us to prosper us, I also establish that God does not want our hearts to be tied in to the wealth He is blessing us with. He wants us to see wealth as a tool.

I used seven or eight passages to establish the initial truth and I will do the same with this. Matthew 6:19-21 says

Don't store up treasures here on earth, where moths eat them and rust destroys them, and where thieves break in and steal. Store your treasures in heaven, where moths and rust cannot destroy, and thieves do not break in and steal. Wherever your treasure is, there the desires of your heart will also be.

The Bible here is not against savings and investments. It cannot be. Wealth is needed to propagate the gospel. Wealth is needed to provide relief in areas of poverty and drought. God loves the poor but He does not like poverty. Poverty can

103

only be combated by wealth along with education which costs money. Matthew 6:21 tells us what the real message is: Where are the desires of your heart? Is your heart in the wealth or is your heart with God? 1 Timothy 6:6-7 says

> Yet true godliness with contentment is itself great wealth. After all, we brought nothing with us when we came into the world, and we can't take anything with us when we leave it. .

Again the message here is quite clear. Where is your focus? Is it on the wealth or is it on eternity? This message is buttressed further in 1 Timothy 6:17-19

> Teach those who are rich in this world not to be proud and not to trust in their money, which is so unreliable. Their trust should be in God, who richly gives us all we need for our enjoyment. Tell them to use their money to do good. They should be rich in good works and generous to those in need, always being ready to share with others. By doing this they will be storing up their treasure as a good foundation for the future so that they may experience true life.

Who is your trust in? In God or in your riches? What are you doing with your wealth? Are you doing good only for yourself or are you being generous?

Matthew 6:33 says

> Seek the Kingdom of God above all else, and live righteously, and he will give you everything you need.

Do we trust God to bless us or are we struggling to make things happen ourselves? Deuteronomy 8:11-17 in the New King James Version further states what God has to say about wealth:

> Beware that you do not forget the LORD your God by not keeping His commandments, His judgments, and His statutes which I command you today, lest—when you have eaten and are full, and have built beautiful houses and dwell in them; and when your herds and your flocks multiply, and your silver and your gold are multiplied, and all that you have is multiplied; when your heart is lifted up, and you forget the LORD your God who brought you out of the land of Egypt, from the house of bondage; who led you through that great and terrible wilderness, in which were fiery serpents and scorpions and thirsty land where there was no water; who brought water for you out of the flinty rock; who fed you in the wilderness with manna, which your fathers did not know, that He might humble you and that He might test you, to do you good in the end— then you say in your heart, 'My power and the might of my hand have gained me this wealth.'

I will share a few more scriptures with you to drive this truth home before we continue.

> No one can serve two masters. For you will hate one and love the other; you will be devoted to one and despise the other. You cannot serve both God and money. *(Matthew 6:24)*

> This is a trustworthy saying: "If someone aspires to be an elder, he desires an honourable position." So an elder must be a man whose life is above reproach. He must be faithful to his wife. He must exercise self-control, live wisely, and have

a good reputation. He must enjoy having guests in his home, and he must be able to teach. He must not be a heavy drinker or be violent. He must be gentle, not quarrelsome, and not love money. *(1 Timothy 3:1-3)*

For the love of money is the root of all kinds of evil. And some people, craving money, have wandered from the true faith and pierced themselves with many sorrows. *(1 Timothy 6:10)*

So we have established two truths. The first is that God wants us to be wealthy. The second is that God does not want our hearts to be corrupted by the wealth. Our hearts must remain focused on God, on doing good and on staying pure.

For the rest of this chapter I want us to focus on and discuss the right disposition to have when using wealth and making purchases. We will look into debt, savings and investments in the next chapter on finances.

Being a good steward of wealth

There are five questions you should ask yourself when seeking to acquire material things. Reflecting on these questions (which should become mind-sets) before you make purchases will enable you to develop the wisdom you need to manage your wealth. In fact, in my experience you are not likely to accumulate significant wealth without developing these mind-sets and if you do, there is a strong likelihood that you will end up spending wrongly. Practicing these mind-sets with small purchases, develops the wisdom required to manage larger more expensive purchases.

Question 1: Why should I buy?

This question like the others will lead to further questions. What is your motive for the purchase? Am I buying because I need it or because I want it? Do I really need this item? Am I trying to impress someone else with this purchase or is the thought genuine?

The process of asking these questions and assessing your honest responses will help you decide whether this material purchase is a good one or a poor one. These questions will apply to the purchase of a house, a car, clothes, shoes and practically anything. For example I see a pair of shoes that I really like. I don't really need a new pair of shoes but I decide to buy them to reward myself for recent hard work. (There is nothing wrong with that unless it is a daily excuse!). I assess myself and I am genuinely not trying to measure up with a work colleague who buys new shoes almost every week so I proceed to the next stage.

Question 2: What should I buy?

Having decided to make the purchase, the next set of questions will arise. Should I buy cheap, good quality or just expensive? Unmarked or designer? Are the shoes I have seen worth the reward I want it for? Could I get better quality shoes elsewhere for a cheaper price? It is rarely a good decision to buy plain cheap. Cheap does not usually last and the quality is poor. Seek to buy good quality products which will last longer as you are more likely to get satisfaction from them.

Question 3: When should I buy?

Do I need to do this now or can it be better purchased at another time? Is there a sale next week which would save me some money or is there one coming up soon? Do I feel pressured to purchase (a bad thing) or would I be comfortable walking away from this place? If you ever feel pressured to buy anything, then don't. Pressured sales are a marketing ploy to make you feel like your world will come to an end if you don't make this purchase here and now.

Question 4: Where should I buy from?

Have I searched for a better deal? Do the sellers have a worthy reputation? What is the aftersales care like? These questions will apply to any item but more specifically to larger goods like cars, garden equipment or home appliances. Who you buy from may make all the difference in aftersales service quality and that may not be necessarily cheap. The point is do your homework and don't just drop the cash.

Question 5: How should I buy?

Should I pay with cash, debit/credit cards; should I buy now and pay later? Can I afford this item now? Do I need to save a bit more? Would using a credit card be wise or am I enslaving myself for a fleeting pleasure? Using credit cards on the whole is generally discouraged, as is the use of store credit due to exorbitant interest rates. There is some value to using a credit card if you will pay it off immediately as it allows you to build a good credit history and also buys you some time before you have to pay the full amount.

By the time you take yourself through these questions honestly and sincerely, only the right purchases will filter through.

Finally in making purchases be sensitive to your spirit.

Not everything that glitters is gold. If it does not feel right, even if looks right or sounds right don't do it! Give yourself more time to make the right decision. By the grace of God, I only make significant purchases when I feel a go-ahead in my spirit. This has saved me from committing to buy things that I would later have regretted. Some years ago, just as we were about to commit to buying a beautiful bungalow, Dami and I felt very uncomfortable in our spirits. We are familiar with walking in the Spirit so we knew something was

God will not desire for us something He has put beyond our reach.

wrong but we really loved the house. It was not exactly what we wanted but it was within budget and was good enough. We prayed and felt the Lord preventing us from going ahead so we called it off.

Shortly after this we found another house. It was slightly more expensive, but we would not have to drive to our daughter's school as it was across the road. The area was peaceful and quiet and it was everything we wanted in a house and much more. We made an offer which was eventually accepted. The lovely couple we purchased the house from had the opportunity to sell it for an extra £35, 000 to someone else but they felt in their hearts that we should have the house so they didn't. They left us with so many things that for months we did not need to purchase cleaning supplies and bulbs as an example. The house was in show home condition. If we had not listened to the Spirit's guidance we would have missed out on God's plan to bless us with this beautiful home.

RIGHT QUESTIONS, RIGHT ANSWERS

1. Why is this Decasection important?

This Decasection is important as we established two truths. God wants us to be wealthy but also God does not want our hearts to be corrupted by wealth

God wants us to be good stewards of the wealth He gives us and we need to assess the cost of any purchase or endeavour by asking ourselves the relevant questions.

2. What must you do to invest in this Decasection of your life? Whatever you do not invest in will depreciate and deteriorate.

We need to regularly review our attitudes to material things in general. Have they taken a hold of our hearts? Are our thoughts predominantly focused on wealth and money or are we focused on God and His work.

DECASECTION

Eight

FINANCIAL

Finances deals with issues about money and how you manage it. Please don't read this chapter without first reading the chapter on the Material Decasection which will give you a foundation. To launch us forward, let us briefly remind ourselves of two significant truths we established in the previous chapter: God wants us to be wealthy but God does not want our hearts to be corrupted by wealth. Matthew 6:24 says

> No one can serve two masters. For you will hate one and love the other; you will be devoted to one and despise the other. You cannot serve both God and money.

We must serve God and use wealth and money for God's purposes. Let me further make this clarification: money is not bad in itself. Money simply takes on the nature of whatever it is used for. If it is used for bad, it is bad and if it is used for good, it is good. A usually bad person can be generous and give money to a friend in need while a usually good person in a moment of weakness, can purchase some cakes with high sugar content when he is supposed to be on a diet. Money is neutral.

The Spiritual Aspect of Money: The Blessing of God

Before we discuss debt, savings and investments I want us to look at the blessing of God. The Bible says in Proverbs 10:22

> The blessing of the LORD makes a person rich, and he adds no sorrow with it.

We all need the blessing of God. There are several ways to ensure the blessing of God upon your life.

The Tithe

The first and most important is the tithe. The tithe is defined as the tenth or ten percent of your gross income. Malachi 3:8-12 says:

> Will a man rob God? Yet you have robbed Me! But you say, 'In what way have we robbed You?' In tithes and offerings. You are cursed with a curse, For you have robbed Me, Even this whole nation.

Bring all the tithes into the storehouse, That there may be food in My house, And try Me now in this," Says the LORD of hosts, "If I will not open for you the windows of heaven And pour out for you such blessing That there will not be room enough to receive it. "And I will rebuke the devourer for your sakes, So that he will not destroy the fruit of your ground, Nor shall the vine fail to bear fruit for you in the field," Says the LORD of hosts; "And all nations will call you blessed, For you will be a delightful land," Says the LORD of hosts. (NKJV)

In this scripture God makes certain things clear which I

will highlight.

1.   Those who do not pay their tithes are robbing God and are bringing a curse upon themselves. (verses 8 and 9).

2.   Those who do pay their tithes will enjoy the windows of Heaven being open resulting in an uncontainable outpouring of blessing. (Verse 10).

3.   The devourer is rebuked when we pay our tithes. (Verse 11a)

4.   Our efforts at work or in life as a whole will be productive when we pay our tithes. (Verse 11b)

5. The results of God's blessing will be evident for all to see. (Verse 12)

The tithe is used for running the church or the ministry you belong to. It is what God has put in place to ensure that His God ordained work does not lack. There are lots of other references to the tithe in the Bible but since many people ask the question of its relevance in the New Testament, I will use a reference from there. In Matthew 23:23 Jesus had this to say:

> What sorrow awaits you teachers of religious law and you Pharisees. Hypocrites! For you are careful to tithe even the tiniest income from your herb gardens, but you ignore the more important aspects of the law — justice, mercy, and faith. You should tithe, yes, but do not neglect the more important things.

Jesus is saying here that the Pharisees were being hypocritical for emphasising money over virtues like justice, mercy and faith; but he did still say paying the tithe is important but not as important as the virtues mentioned. Let

113

me also share a reference on tithing from before the days of the law. In Genesis 14:17-20

> After Abram returned from his victory over Kedorlaomer and all his allies, the king of Sodom went out to meet him in the valley of Shaveh (that is, the King's Valley). And Melchizedek, the king of Salem and a priest of God Most High, brought Abram some bread and wine. Melchizedek blessed Abram with this blessing: "Blessed be Abram by God Most High, Creator of heaven and earth. And blessed be God Most High, who has defeated your enemies for you." Then Abram gave Melchizedek a tenth of all the goods he had recovered.

This scripture from the Old Testament is from before the law was instituted. Abram the father of faith paid tithes to the priest of the most High God.

Charitable Offerings

This refers to gifts of money or other form of substance to people or causes. Giving in this way also releases the blessing of God into our lives. Luke 6:38 says

> Give, and you will receive. Your gift will return to you in full—pressed down, shaken together to make room for more, running over, and poured into your lap. The amount you give will determine the amount you get back.

There are three main categories of offerings:

Giving to the less privileged: This is obviously the main one: giving to people in need or who do not have enough. It encourages a generous heart when we engage in this. Our giving does not have to be monetary; it could be clothes, dry food or other items. Psalm 41:1-3 and Proverbs 19:17 say respectively

> Oh, the joys of those who are kind to the poor! The LORD rescues them when they are in trouble. The LORD protects them and keeps them alive. He gives them prosperity in the land and rescues them from their enemies. The LORD nurses them when they are sick and restores them to health.

> If you help the poor, you are lending to the LORD — and he will repay you!

It's so good to know that God honours us when we help the less privileged.

Giving to worthy causes: This is another form of giving that attracts God's blessing. In this day and age there are various charitable causes we can contribute to depending on what interests we have or what tugs on the mercy strings of our hearts. In the Old Testament during the building of the tabernacle, the people were encouraged to give. They recognised that without God they would not have any substance so they were willing and gave freely.

> And Moses spake unto all the congregation of the children of Israel, saying, This is the thing which the LORD commanded, saying, Take ye from among you an offering unto the LORD: whosoever is of a willing heart, let him bring it, an offering of the LORD; gold, and silver, and brass.(*Exodus 35:4-5, KJV*)

> And all the congregation of the children of Israel departed from the presence of Moses. And they came, every one

whose heart stirred him up, and every one whom his spirit made willing, and they brought the LORD's offering to the work of the tabernacle of the congregation, and for all his service, and for the holy garments. And they came, both men and women, as many as were willing hearted, and brought bracelets, and earrings, and rings, and tablets, all jewels of gold: and every man that offered offered an offering of gold unto the LORD. *(Exodus 35: 20-22, KJV)*

The children of Israel brought a willing offering unto the LORD, every man and woman, whose heart made them willing to bring for all manner of work, which the LORD had commanded to be made by the hand of Moses. *(Exodus 35: 29, KJV)*

Can you see how many times the Bible used the phrase willing? We are to give willingly, not by obligation, pressure or compulsion. We should not feel bullied to give but rather we should give out of understanding.

Giving in appreciation: This form of giving can be directed towards parents, church leaders, those who have helped us in one way or another, senior or junior colleagues at work. We are to give in appreciation to those who have parental influence over us, spiritual leaders, people who have been kind to us and the people we work with. Even if you do not feel your parents are entitled to nor need anything, remember that God commands us to honour our parents. (See the chapter on family and the section on parents).

How to Give

In all your giving, you must do so liberally with a willing and cheerful heart. 2 Corinthians 9:6-8 says

> Remember this—a farmer who plants only a few seeds will get a small crop. But the one who plants generously will get a generous crop. You must each decide in your heart how much to give. And don't give reluctantly or in response to pressure. "For God loves a person who gives cheerfully." And God will generously provide all you need. Then you will always have everything you need and plenty left over to share with others.

Practical Aspects of Money

Having dealt with the spiritual aspect of money, we need to look at the practical aspects of money. This is extremely important to help us manage our finances properly. The first thing you must do when practically assessing your finances is turn the light on! Nothing must be hidden in the dark. Pull out your bank statements, bring them up online, lay them out before you; you must know what you earn, what you own, what you owe and how you plan to grow.

Your Financial State is the sum total of the four things mentioned above: What you earn, own, owe and your plan to grow. What you own can be material or financial but it is likely that what you owe is just financial.

Earn (income)

How much do you earn? Are you being paid what you are worth? How can you boost your earning power? Have you explored getting a better job? Have you considered developing yourself further to improve your earning potential? Have you considered if a change in career may suit you better and earn you more? Have you thought of getting a part time job once or twice a week in addition to your regular job instead of just vegetating in front of the television daily?

These are questions you may need to keep asking yourself and challenging yourself with until you start to get satisfactory answers and are motivated to do something more productive.

Own (savings and possessions)

This refers to things you have bought and paid for. What do you actually own? Are the things you consider yours still on a payment plan? If they are, you should move them to the owe section as they are not yet properly yours. This includes your mortgage unless you have paid it off.

Owe (debt)

This refers to things that you have but are yet to complete payment for. This includes loans, credit cards, store cards and obviously your mortgage if you have one. Debt is a big problem all over the world but especially in developed areas where credit facilities are easily available. The benefits of credit facilities are good and enable people to get things they need but cannot yet afford, but the downside is the lack of control which results in more and more borrowing until the debt becomes a burden.

> *Money is not bad in itself. Money simply takes on the nature of whatever it is used for.*

In December 2013 the amount of personal debt in the UK stood at £1.435 Trillion! The mortgage figure was £1.277 Trillion. This means that non mortgage debt stands at £158.1 Billion! Staggering you might say but the result of this debt is that every 5 minutes and 3 seconds someone is made bankrupt, and every 18 minutes and 15 seconds a property is repossessed! We need to stop! We need to stop borrowing! We need to develop a repayment plan.

See what the Bible has to say about borrowing in the following scriptures.

Just as the rich rule the poor, so the borrower is servant to the lender. *(Proverbs 22:7)*

The LORD your God will bless you as he has promised. You will lend money to many nations but will never need to borrow. You will rule many nations, but they will not rule over you. *(Deuteronomy 15:6)*

The LORD will send rain at the proper time from his rich treasury in the heavens and will bless all the work you do. You will lend to many nations, but you will never need to borrow from them. *(Deuteronomy 28:12)*

Can we get to that place in which we refuse to be servants of the system and refrain from borrowing? Yes it is possible. The only type of borrowing that might be somewhat acceptable is having a mortgage. It makes sense to live in a property which is gradually becoming yours than giving a monthly donation to a landlord for the privilege of living in his house. Having said that let us learn to live within our means, avoid debt and credit cards and believe the Lord to take us higher and higher in our finances.

Grow (investments)

This refers to structures you have put in place to grow your finances. This could be in the form of savings, investments, property, shares or even a business which you are doing on the side. I mentioned earlier on about getting a second job if you need some extra money, that could be a business instead, something that you can grow. I know several people who work for shops like Marks and Spencer's, the Post Office and other large organisations that recruit extra staff around Christmas in order to boost their finances at that time of the year.

I want to share with you a few principles behind investments as I round up this chapter. In Genesis 26:1-4 and 12-14 there is a story of a man called Isaac who invested. The principles we learn from this scripture are invaluable.

> A severe famine now struck the land, as had happened before in Abraham's time. So Isaac moved to Gerar, where Abimelech, king of the Philistines, lived. The LORD appeared to Isaac and said, "Do not go down to Egypt, but do as I tell you. Live here as a foreigner in this land, and I will be with you and bless you. I hereby confirm that I will give all these lands to you and your descendants, just as I solemnly promised Abraham, your father. I will cause your descendants to become as numerous as the stars of the sky, and I will give them all these lands. And through your descendants all the nations of the earth will be blessed.
>
> When Isaac planted his crops that year, he harvested a hundred times more grain than he planted, for the LORD blessed him. He became a very rich man, and his wealth

continued to grow. He acquired so many flocks of sheep and goats, herds of cattle, and servants that the Philistines became jealous of him.

Principle 1: Divine Location. Where has God planted you? Location is everything. There is a place God wants you to invest. Even if it looks barren, if that is where you are being directed to, if your research shows it up as a good place to invest, go for it but do your homework.

Principle 2: Diversification. Isaac planted crops but grew rich in sheep, goats and cattle. Don't put all your investment eggs in one basket, diversify. Have some savings, some investments, some property and some shares. Have a foundational base then you can invest heavily in your area of interest like Isaac did. He moved from crops to different kinds of husbandry.

Principle 3: Don't borrow to invest. BIG MISTAKE. Never borrow to invest no matter how fantastic the scheme looks. It is usually a mistake to borrow for an investment. You invest with disposable income, something you can afford to lose.

Principle 4: Beware of get rich quick scams. Any investment that will make you a millionaire almost overnight is to be considered suspicious. Have you ever wondered why people would be so eager to inform everyone of a money making venture that will make them millions? It does not really add up to me. Many of these people get rich, telling others how to get rich but are not getting rich themselves using those same ideas or principles. If something looks odd, it probably is!

Principle 5: Growth is gradual. Have a long term plan;

growth is gradual so prepare for the long haul.

Principle 6: Get a good financial adviser. Isaac had the best financial advice. His adviser projected that although there was a famine in the land, the situation created certain opportunities of its own. His adviser told him to stay when others were going and it was worth listening to the advice. Who are you listening to for financial advice? Isaac listened to God but God has also equipped some people with knowledge. Get good advice!

Principle 7: Get life insurance and maybe even income protection. One of my pastors once said, 'If you have a family and you do not have life insurance, you are a criminal' I will add to that and suggest that you should seriously consider income protection. If for any reason you cannot work (God forbid), your family's finances are protected and with life insurance, your family is protected if you are no longer here.

There is a story in 2 Kings 4:1-7 which you might find interesting. I will only include verse 1 here for our purpose:

> One day the widow of a member of the group of prophets came to Elisha and cried out, "My husband who served you is dead, and you know how he feared the LORD. But now a creditor has come, threatening to take my two sons as slaves.

This good man was unfortunately in debt as many people are but he had left no provision for his family in the event of his death. In those days, if you could not pay your debts, your possessions, your children and even your spouse would be sold into slavery to make up the amount owed. Lesson? Don't be in debt but also make provision for your family in the event of you no longer being here.

RIGHT QUESTIONS, RIGHT ANSWERS

1. Why is this Decasection important?

Your money is your life as you spend the most productive hours of the day and your life working for it. Your attitude to money is important. You need to understand it properly.

There is a spiritual side to money but also a practical side to money. Both are important and one should not be neglected over the other.

2. What must you do to invest in this Decasection of your life? Whatever you do not invest in will depreciate and deteriorate.

Hopefully you have a source of income. If not, then that is the first place to start. Seek to be gainfully employed or run your own business. If you already have one then ensure you are walking in the spiritual aspect of money by paying your tithes and giving offerings. However you need to ask yourself a question: do you actually understand the spiritual basis of tithing and giving offerings? If you don't then invest some time in this area by studying the scriptures on the subject or reviewing what I have discussed. Also ask God to help you implement this.

You also need to work towards increasing your earning power, knowing what you own and working on reducing your debt. Finally, put something in place to grow your money. Think about your money working for you, not just you working for money.

Nine

FAMILY

This refers to your nuclear and extended families. It goes without saying that your nuclear family will take preference over your extended family but you still have a responsibility to your parents and siblings and we will look into that here. Psalm 68:6a says

'God sets the solitary in families...'

Nuclear family

Your nuclear family consists of your spouse and children. We have already discussed marriage so let us look at the area of children.

Why have children? How many children should I have? What do I do with them? These and many other questions usually plague the mind of those who start to consider having children. I believe a couple should have children because they want them, not because they feel society want them to have children. Society will not bring up your children for you so you should not feel pressured by others in to having them. Children are supposed to be a blessing from God not a burden. If you look to Heaven and offer thanksgiving at the news that you are expecting a child, that is good. If your response is a negative one then maybe you ought to have been more careful.

I also believe children should be born into a stable loving family. Children should not be used to heal a rift between couples, neither should they be used as bargaining chips. If a couple are unmarried or going through a rough patch, all plans to have children should be suspended.

It takes great commitment and dedication to bring up children and if you are not prepared to take the step to commit to one another then you are not likely to be sufficiently committed to bring up children. The vast majority of juvenile delinquents, child criminals, bullies and those who start smoking and doing drugs in their early teens come from unstable homes either in which there is only one parent or where the relationship was already breaking down. This is not to make single parents feel uncomfortable; many of them will agree that their situation is not the ideal one for child upbringing. The full compliment of skills required for the effective upbringing of children is challenging enough for a couple to have, talk less of a single parent.

Children should be planned and prepared for. They should only be brought into the world when you believe you are (or soon will be) in a position to give them what they will need to have a good, comfortable life and eventually grow up to be responsible members of society. If you don't feel you are able to forecast that position of emotional and financial security in your own life for whatever reason then do not proceed with having children. There are enough pressures in life to cope with, adding child rearing to the mix if you are unprepared can and has tipped many into depression and results in many considering termination of pregnancy.

I believe every child has a mission and a purpose. That goes without saying as we have already established that from our chapter on Purpose. What is actually more important is for every parent to know that it is their responsibility to help their child find their purpose in life and help them to develop in that direction according to Proverbs 22:6:

> Direct your children onto the right path, and when they are older, they will not leave it.

It is our responsibility as parents to direct our children onto the right path. Until they reach a certain age and even beyond that, their lives will be defined by your parenting. They will be described as your children for as long as you live, so you are majorly responsible for what happens to them, good or bad.

The right path can be looked at in two main ways:

The first way is the right path of spirituality and morality, to help them become good, responsible, spiritual and moral members of society. Children learn primarily from what they see so we should direct them primarily by showcasing life as it should be lived, recognising that whatever positive or negative behaviour we display in front of our children will probably find its way into their lives.

The second way is the right path of educational development which should encompass vocational development and purpose. Are they heading in the right direction or have they missed it somewhere along the line?

Skills required for bringing up children

I will first discuss the relevant skills needed to bring up children generally then I will look at what we need as parents to help direct our children onto a vocational path. Please read the following passage.

> So I say, let the Holy Spirit guide your lives. Then you won't be doing what your sinful nature craves. The sinful nature wants to do evil, which is just the opposite of what the Spirit wants. And the Spirit gives us desires that are the opposite of what the sinful nature desires. These two forces are constantly fighting each other, so you are not free to carry out your good intentions. But when you are directed by the Spirit, you are not under obligation to the Law of Moses. When you follow the desires of your sinful nature, the results are very clear: sexual immorality, impurity, lustful pleasures, idolatry, sorcery, hostility, quarreling, jealousy, outbursts of anger, selfish ambition, dissension, division, envy, drunkenness, wild parties, and other sins like these. Let me tell you again, as I have before, that anyone living that sort of life will not inherit the Kingdom of God. But the Holy Spirit produces this kind of fruit in our lives: love, joy, peace, patience, kindness, goodness, faithfulness, gentleness, and self-control. There is no law against these things! Those who belong to Christ Jesus have nailed the passions and desires of their sinful nature to his cross and crucified them there. Since we are living by the Spirit, let us follow the Spirit's leading in every part of our lives. Let us

not become conceited, or provoke one another, or be jealous of one another. *(Galatians 5:16-26)*

If you were ever unsure about needing the help of the Holy Spirit in your life, you will cry out to Him when it comes to bringing up children! There are two parts to the scripture above: the first part which talks about all the negative things we should not be doing but which our sinful nature would want to do and the second part which talks about the fruit of the Spirit. Please note that the Holy Spirit will produce the fruit in you. In other words He will not bestow or impart, He will produce. This means that it is a process of development.

Essentially the skills you need for bringing up children are the fruit of the Spirit.

Love: You will need bucket loads of love. Children need to feel loved even when they are being disciplined, they need to be aware that love is the real root of the discipline. If you really love your children you will not only provide them with lots of hugs, kisses and cuddles but also lots of discipline when appropriate. A few months after we had our second daughter, our first one came to sit beside me one day and asked, 'Daddy do you love me?' I immediately knew what the problem was and answering Yes was not going to solve it. I hugged her and explained that we still loved her as much as we ever did but as her sister was so young she needed a lot more attention. From that day we regularly told her how much we loved her to reassure her. Children need to feel loved.

Joy: Joy is infectious but so is moodiness. In the chapter on your mental life I stated that 'Depressed people depress people'. If you want your children to grow up happy, be a happy person.

Peace: Too many children grow up in troubled environments which results in them living troubled lives. A peaceful environment will allow children to express themselves freely, telling you good, bad and ugly things. This knowledge will help you to become aware of what your children are being exposed to and help you manage their concerns better. If you don't know because they won't say, you will be dangerously ignorant.

Patience: Children are still children. You were never perfect and neither are they. Be patient with them. Yes be firm, but be patient. When you are tempted to blow your top remember the good words of Jesus from Matthew 7:3-5

> And why worry about a speck in your friend's eye when you have a log in your own? How can you think of saying to your friend, 'Let me help you get rid of that speck in your eye,' when you can't see past the log in your own eye? Hypocrite! First get rid of the log in your own eye; then you will see well enough to deal with the speck in your friend's eye.

The point of this scripture is simple. Whatever complaint you have to pick with your children, remember you have your own weaknesses. Before you get on your high horse, remember you are not perfect. Does that mean we should let things slide as parents since we are not perfect? No. It does however mean we should be more tolerant of other people's mistakes because we realise we are not perfect.

Kindness: Children are sensitive and will reproduce your actions. Be kind to them and they will grow up kind individuals

Goodness: This refers to a sweet disposition, a good heart, a warm personality. This always reassures children and allows them to thrive.

Faithfulness: This refers to dedication and commitment which we will need to be when bringing up children.

Gentleness: Children need gentleness not harshness, brute force, or aggression.

Self-control: This is extremely important especially if you are given to anger or are emotionally depleted due to other issues of life. You may find yourself losing control with your children but having self-control will enable you manage challenges more effectively. As a rule do not act, speak or make important decisions when you are angry.

Ephesians 4:26-27 says

And "don't sin by letting anger control you." Don't let the sun go down while you are still angry, for anger gives a foothold to the devil.

You don't want the devil having a foothold. This is when violence against children, emotional and physical abuse and other forms of abuse set in. You are angry they have done something naughty which you warned them not to do; so you decide to find a way to really hurt them. Sometimes even worse, they have done nothing but their other parent has. So to hurt your spouse, partner or ex, you hurt the children. This is totally wrong and completely unacceptable. You definitely need self- control.

If you find that you lack any of these virtues, seek help,

first from God, then from other forms of support like family members, church family, even social services if appropriate. What I find most interesting about the skills required for bringing up children is that they are the same skills required for interacting with people. It is all about having people skills and learning to manage difficult people. (Children can be difficult people!)

It is also important to note that working on yourself to become a better person will result in you being a better parent. The more of the fruit of the Spirit you have, the better a person you will be. You will also be better at interacting with others, children included.

Education (academic, pastoral care, extra-curricular)

Every child needs an education. Whether it is through formal education, that is attending a school or being home schooled, all children need to be educated. In modern society unlike many years ago, both male and female children can go to school. There are still some parts of the world where this is still a struggle but the situation is generally getting better across the world. Sadly in some places, educational provision is getting worse.

In choosing a school for your children there are at least three things to consider.

Academic: Will this school provide my child with the relevant academic background to compete in today's world?

Children should be planned and prepared for.

It is no longer enough to just attend any old school down the road. The school your child goes to will, to a general extent, determine the direction your child's life will go. Please note that I stated 'to a general extent'. There will be exceptions as there are always exceptions in life, but please do your personal research. Not all schools are equal. If they were, there would be no league tables as you have in the UK and in many other countries. Some schools consistently perform better than others giving your child a better opportunity for a better start in life. Before you enrol your child in a school, make enquiries; compare schools and work towards having your child attend the best school possible.

Pastoral Care: Will this school provide my child with the relevant pastoral care that will re-enforce the values I have so painstakingly introduced into my child at home?

We moved across two or three boroughs in London to get close to the school we wanted our daughter to go to. This is not uncommon. In fact many surveys have shown that one of the commonest reasons for moving house among young families is to get close to good schools. We loved the environment we lived in at the time, we had great neighbours, our little cul-de-sac was warm and friendly, our house was close to our local church but the schools were not great academically. One can say there is always extra tuition but that was not the real problem. The real problem was the kind of foul language spoken by the children in the schools at such a young age! We determined there was no way we would allow our child to go to those schools and we had to move. What kind of pastoral care is provided by the school? Do they even care about behaviour or are they just focused on academic performance?

Extra-curricular activities: Will this school provide my child with the right mix of extra-curricular activities to make my child a balanced individual?

A strong extra-curricular background is important to help children become rounded and balanced in life. Sports and music help children develop and interact while providing them with avenues to expend energy, exert themselves and develop talents. A good school must provide a range of extra-curricular activities that will expose your children to abilities they did not know they had. Not all boys will play football and not all girls will do ballet but all children will find something they enjoy and your chosen school should help them discover this. Remember it is your responsibility as a parent to facilitate all of this and sometimes finding the right school may be all the hard work you need.

Extended Family

This consists of all your family members not included in your nuclear family. This list is topped by your parents and then your siblings. This is then followed by uncles, aunties, cousins and this can stretch on and on. In this section I will look primarily at your relationship with your parents and touch briefly on your relationship with your siblings.

Your Parents

This refers primarily to your biological parents but could also apply to anyone who has brought you up or has parental responsibility over you. If you were orphaned at a very young age, your parents are the people who have played the parental role in your life. Exodus 20:12 says

Honor your father and mother. Then you will live a long, full life in the land the Lord your God is giving you.

The word of God is clear. We are to honour our father and mother. It is one of the Ten Commandments. Paul the apostle expands further in Ephesians 6:1-3:

Children, obey your parents because you belong to the Lord, for this is the right thing to do. "Honour your father and mother." This is the first commandment with a promise: If you honour your father and mother, "things will go well for you, and you will have a long life on the earth."

The Bible says honouring our parents is the right thing to do. By obeying this commandment things will go well for us and we will have a long life on earth. This commandment is not only to those who have good parents. This commandment is not only to those who have kind parents. This commandment is not only to those who have responsible parents. This commandment is to all of us. Those of us with wicked and unkind parents; those of us with parents involved in the occult; those of us whose parents have problems with drugs and alcohol; those of us whose parents abused us in one way or another. God said honour your parents.

Let me be clear in stating that this does not mean keep exposing yourself to danger or follow their advice if it is contrary to God or common sense. To honour means to regard, to respect or to esteem. Respecting your parents was a very big thing in the days of the Old Testament. You can see this from the following scriptures in Exodus 21:15, 17

Anyone who strikes father or mother must be put to death.

135

Anyone who dishonours father or mother must be put to death.

Fortunately we do not have such drastic laws today but I showed these to explain how important it is to honour your parents. So what does it actually mean in practical terms apart from not hitting them?

Jesus explained it even better in Matthew 15:4-6 when he was disputing with the religious leaders of his day.

> For instance, God says, 'Honour your father and mother,' and 'Anyone who speaks disrespectfully of father or mother must be put to death.' But you say it is all right for people to say to their parents, 'Sorry, I can't help you. For I have vowed to give to God what I would have given to you.' In this way, you say they don't need to honour their parents. And so you cancel the word of God for the sake of your own tradition.

From what Jesus said, to honour your parents involves helping them, supporting them, giving to them. It is easy to do this if they are seemingly worthy of the honour you should give them. The real problem comes when you feel they don't deserve the honour you should give them. Why then should you still honour them? Several reasons:

1. It is the commandment of God. That on its own should settle it. Not only is it a commandment but it is one that comes with a promise; that it may be well with you. Remember that without them you wouldn't exist. They are God's instrument for bringing you into this world and although they may have failed in their responsibility in bringing you up, they are still

your parents and God said to honour them.

2. Whatever you sow, you will also reap. Even if your parents don't deserve your honour and support, sowing good seeds will result in you reaping a good harvest.

3. Honour your parents and your children will honour you. Remember that you want to model the life you want your children to live.

4. Parental Spiritual Influence. Due to the position your parents occupy in your life, they exert some spiritual influence over you. If they bless you, you are blessed but if they curse you with good reason, you will struggle unless God intervenes and has mercy on you. This is why I recommend that you seek parental blessing before significant events in your life like marriage. It is important you win them over to your side due to the spiritual influence they have over you. This is so important that I have dedicated the next section to it. This will open your eyes as you will start to understand why certain things have happened to you.

Parental Spiritual Influence

My people are destroyed for lack of knowledge. *(Hosea 4:6a, NKJV)*

I have discovered certain things in my observation of the patterns of people's lives. We are much more influenced by our parents than we think. To be more precise, we are more spiritually influenced by our parents than we could ever imagine. We have all met people who excuse their temperaments by saying things like 'I am like my father, he had a bad temper' or 'I am like my mother, she was very quiet'. Unfortunately your parents have passed on a lot more than that to you even without their knowing.

Most men who have struggles with sexual immorality in one form or another had parents who were either polygamous, unfaithful or had their own struggles with sexual immorality. In fact I have come to the conclusion that most men of African background will have some form of internal or external struggle with sexual immorality due to our heritage in polygamy and infidelity. Many of you have asked questions and wonder why you do the things you do. The answer for many is that their parents walked that path and they are unwittingly walking the same path.

Many children of alcoholics become alcoholics even though they hated their parents for being alcoholics. Many children of unfaithful fathers become unfaithful even though they hated what their father did to their mother. What is responsible for this pattern? I call it Parental Spiritual Influence. Your parents exert spiritual influence on your life whether you know it or not.

Let me explain it in another way: we all have our personal demons to fight. Whatever personal demons you don't overcome will face your children. Children will be forced to fight the battles their parents were unable to win. They will therefore have their battles and that of their parents to fight unless something is done about it.

From the day God opened my eyes to this revelation, I have taken my life and my 'personal demons' more seriously. Now for some of you, your personal demons may be nothing more than, a touch of laziness or being too laidback about life, but for others, if you look into your family and see for example that your parents were divorced, then you notice that many of your siblings are getting divorced or have other marital struggles and you then start to have problems yourself; then you can be sure that unless you remedy the situation your children will face the same struggles.

For others it may be financial. Your parents were bad with money and now you find that you always seem to have financial problems. It is time to deal with it. If you don't, your children will start to have the same struggles.

> *Whatever you sow, you will also reap.*

What can you do about negative Parental Spiritual Influence?

1. Recognise God as your primary Father and invite His spiritual influence into your life.

2. Be aware of what is happening to you and deal with it. Pray against it, work against it and if necessary get people to agree with you in prayer against it

3. Start to pray for your children. Pray for them, equip them and train them to defeat the issue that you have had to fight be it marital, financial, educational or moral.

Siblings: In the next chapter on friendships and relationships I look into how to comport yourself with people in general and this will cover relating with your siblings.

RIGHT QUESTIONS, RIGHT ANSWERS

1. Why is this Decasection important?

This Decasection is important because it looks at your children who are your future. It is your responsibility to direct them onto the right path that God wants them to go spiritually, morally and educationally.

This Decasection shows that the fruit of the Spirit are the essential to bring up children. Becoming a better person will make you a better parent. You must choose schools wisely to reflect what you want for your children with respect to academic work, pastoral care and extra-curricular activities.

Parental honour and support is a commandment. Be aware of the possibility of negative Parental Spiritual Influence and the effect it may already be having on you.

2. What must you do to invest in this Decasection of your life? Whatever you do not invest in will depreciate and deteriorate.

You must be walking in the fruit of the Spirit to become a better person, a better parent and a better child to your parents. You must support your parents enough as they get older (emotionally, financially and otherwise).

Regularly review the progress of your children in life and in school. Carry out this review with them so they feel involved in the process.

Do something about negative Parental Spiritual Influence. Identify them, pray against them and pray for your children.

Ten

FRIENDSHIP AND RELATIONSHIPS

This is the last of the Decasections to be addressed. It is easy to start to assume that you can do it all by yourself but no man is an island. In fact looking through scripture, God makes it clear He does not want man to be alone. In Genesis 2:18a God says

> "Then the Lord God said, "It is not good for the man to be alone..."

It is not good for man to be alone. God does not want us to be lone rangers. Psalm 68:6a also says

> God places the lonely in families...

God is looking for people to be absorbed into a community where they can experience all that God has for them. That is partly where the church community comes in. The church is a place where God intends for us to develop strong healthy relationships. Unfortunately many people find themselves being hurt in church because a few basic scriptural principles are not being followed.

1 Corinthians 12 likens the body of Christ to an actual body

with many parts. No part can function effectively without the other. We are interdependent on each other. Individual 'cells' working together as a system or organ for an ultimate purpose.

There are three types of relationships I want to address initially. They are General, Gender and Greater relationships.

General Relationships: This refers to our relationships with people in general. Ephesians 4:29-32 says

> Don't use foul or abusive language. Let everything you say be good and helpful, so that your words will be an encouragement to those who hear them. And do not bring sorrow to God's Holy Spirit by the way you live. Remember, he has identified you as his own, guaranteeing that you will be saved on the day of redemption. Get rid of all bitterness, rage, anger, harsh words, and slander, as well as all types of evil behaviour. Instead, be kind to each other, tenderhearted, forgiving one another, just as God through Christ has forgiven you.

Romans 12:18 says

> Do all that you can to live in peace with everyone.

And also Galatians 6:10 records

> Therefore, whenever we have the opportunity, we should do good to everyone—especially to those in the family of faith.

We should be nice to each other, the Bible says tender-hearted. Many people get angry too easily, they are rude, insulting and annoying. This is contrary to being a true worshiper. The Bible says we should put away bitterness, anger, rage and harsh words. We should be tender-hearted and forgiving. We should live at peace and do good to all men but especially believers. People won't like you if you are always frowning, unhappy or looking like you are sucking lemons. Change your attitude to life. Be a joyful believer. Be accepting of other peoples limitations.

Some people are very quick to criticise the flaws in others. Jesus said in Matthew 7:3-5

> And why worry about a speck in your friend's eye when you have a log in your own? How can you think of saying to your friend, 'Let me help you get rid of that speck in your eye,' when you can't see past the log in your own eye? Hypocrite! First get rid of the log in your own eye; then you will see well enough to deal with the speck in your friend's eye.

The truth is that many people with these negative tendencies often have a need for healing in their own lives. Bitter people make people bitter and those who are hurt, hurt others. We will look at this in a bit more detail later on.

Gender Relationships: This refers to our relationships with the opposite sex. 1 Timothy 5:1-2 says

> Never speak harshly to an older man, but appeal to him respectfully as you would to your own father. Talk to younger men as you would to your own brothers. Treat older women as you would your mother, and treat younger women with all purity as you would your own sisters.

Ephesians 5:3-7 also says

Let there be no sexual immorality, impurity, or greed among you. Such sins have no place among God's people. Obscene stories, foolish talk, and coarse jokes—these are not for you. Instead, let there be thankfulness to God. You can be sure that no immoral, impure, or greedy person will inherit the Kingdom of Christ and of God. For a greedy person is an idolater, worshiping the things of this world. Don't be fooled by those who try to excuse these sins, for the anger of God will fall on all who disobey him. Don't participate in the things these people do.

Sexual immorality is on the increase. It is becoming rife and the Bible says it should not be named among us. If you have been engaging in sexual immorality which for the purpose of this section I would define as sexual dealings with a person other than your spouse, it is not right; it is not acceptable for a true worshiper of God. Stop it!

Let us look at Ephesians 5:5-8 from The Amplified version:

For be sure of this: that no person practicing sexual vice or impurity in thought or in life, or one who is covetous [who has lustful desire for the property of others and is greedy for gain]—for he [in effect] is an idolater—has any inheritance in the kingdom of Christ and of God. Let no one delude and deceive you with empty excuses and groundless arguments [for these sins], for through these things the wrath of God comes upon the sons of rebellion and disobedience. So do not associate or be sharers with them. For once you were darkness, but now you are light in the Lord; walk as children of Light [lead the lives of those native-born to the Light].

If you have found yourself in an inappropriate relationship

with the opposite sex then you need to make adjustments. How do I know a relationship with the opposite sex is inappropriate?

- If I have a very close special relationship with someone of the opposite sex and I have no plans to marry that person, I am probably too close and I have probably overstepped some boundaries.

- Even if we are planning to marry and we are engaging in some form of activity (sexual or para-sexual) that cannot be discussed freely in a Christian public setting then we have probably overstepped some boundaries.

- If we have started to live together before we are officially married then we have probably overstepped some boundaries.

Now I have been very careful to use the word 'probably'. The whole idea is for you to examine yourself and if you are uncomfortable with your closeness then do something about it before it is too late. No one is beyond sexual immorality so put some safeguards in place and save yourself from pain. Being a spiritual person, being a worker in church or holding a church leadership position does not confer immunity against sexual immorality. We will deal with the solution to this in more detail later.

Greater Relationships: This refers to connecting with people who are 'greater' than us or ahead of us in the game of life. It is extremely important in your career, in your ministry, in your marriage and in life as a whole that you connect with people who are ahead of you in the game of life. How do you identify these people? These are people who have been where

145

you are and are where you want to end up. They are not just people you admire or people you like. They are people who have been where you are and are where you want to end up. A lot of people will refer to this as mentoring. Mentoring is good, it is fantastic but as in everything in life there must be safeguards.

For those of us who are mentors we must never position ourselves as the final authority in anyone's life because we are not. Only God is. We are to give good, sensible, and spiritual, Bible based advice which we should expect them to also check out for themselves.

For those of us who are being mentored you must never position anyone in your life as the final authority. Only God has the final say. You must be submissive, have a learner's heart but always check everything you are told with the word of God. In my experience, many Christians from African backgrounds accept the 'word of the prophets' or men of God in their lives without question; hook, line and sinker. That is unscriptural. Acts 17:10-11 says

> That very night the believers sent Paul and Silas to Berea. When they arrived there, they went to the Jewish synagogue. And the people of Berea were more open-minded than those in Thessalonica, and they listened eagerly to Paul's message. They searched the Scriptures day after day to see if Paul and Silas were teaching the truth.

1 John 4:1 says

> Dear friends, do not believe everyone who claims to speak by the Spirit. You must test them to see if the spirit they have

comes from God. For there are many false prophets in the world.

The Berean Christians were open minded, another translation says 'noble'. The Amplified version uses the phrase better disposed. Why? They received the word AND checked and searched to see if what they were told is correct. Who preached to them? Apostle Paul. But they still verified what they were being told with the scriptures and they were described as honourable. Having a mentor is not meant to replace God in your life, it is simply a means to access information in a few hours that would otherwise have taken you many years and many mistakes to learn. So please connect with people who are ahead of you in the game of life but please accept responsibility for every word or piece of advice you incorporate into your life.

Now in choosing people whom you will permit to speak into your life, either as mentors or friends; there are at least two kinds of people you need to be careful of.

1. Ungodly people. The Bible says just by avoiding certain people you are blessed. Psalm 1:1 says:

Oh, the joys of those who do not follow the advice of the wicked, or stand around with sinners, or join in with mockers.

1 Corinthians 15:33 says

Don't be fooled by those who say such things, for "bad company corrupts good character."

There is no easy way to put it: you need to be careful of ungodly people and ensure they don't influence you

147

negatively. This is especially important for young people. I have discovered that there is no such thing as a static relationship - you are either influencing someone or being influenced by someone. I once had a friend I used to play tennis with but he was always talking about how he was chasing women; some married, some single, he wasn't really bothered. I think he was trying to impress me as guys do. But very quickly I realised that if I did not say or do anything I would start to think I was missing out on life by being married (that's what will happen with time).

I needed to be clear about who was influencing who, so I started to talk actively about Christianity, why fooling around was bad even if you are not a Christian, how much I was enjoying being a one-woman man and how marriage is so sweet. Eventually he stopped bragging about his conquests and started confiding in me, asking for marriage advice, how to choose a good wife and what to look for in a woman. So, the balance of influence changed. Rather than me starting to think I was losing out on life by being married, (because I was hearing all this seemingly exciting single life style) he started to realise he was on the wrong path. The point is: there is no static relationship, you are either influencing or being influenced.

2. Godly people who are not heading in your direction. Some people are good people, godly people even, but they are not going in the same direction as you. A pastor once said, the fact that two things are good does not mean they go together. That's why you don't add salt to your tea or sugar to your stew. When you start to critically assess and evaluate your associations, some of those that will be affected will be good

godly people who are simply going in a different direction from you. God will replace them with other people who will lead you in the right direction. If you maintain strong ties with people who are not heading in your direction, you may find yourself being distracted from your focus. This is relevant in business, in Christian ministry, in your career and in education.

When I was in medical school, especially in the early stages, it was difficult to have close friends from other disciplines who did not study as intensively as we did as Medics. Very quickly I learnt to hook up with people who could understand why I was reading so much and we herded each other in the same direction. Remember, they are not bad people, just good people going in a different direction. If you are trying to make headway in your profession, business or ministry, you need to be hanging around people with similar passions and interests so you can herd and shepherd each other towards similar goals.

So who is a friend?

A friend is an individual who over time, has earned your trust and your closeness by virtue of you having some form of a relationship in which you have gotten to know each other. You can be yourself with your friend. There are five operative words in that definition. We have:

The time factor: Don't rush into close friendships. Allow them to develop over time.

The trust factor: You must be able to trust your friend but trust should be progressively earned. If your friend does not pass the trust test at one level you cannot expect him to be dependable at a higher level. Don't place demands on people beyond what they are prepared to commit to.

The closeness factor: There must be an element of proximity or you would not be friends. It is difficult to maintain long distance friendships but I am aware that some people may have contrary views to this.

The knowledge factor: You must know each other fairly well and that knowledge becomes progressive as you spend more and more time together.

The relationship factor: What is the basis of your friendship? It usually starts somewhere such as being volunteers in the same charity, tennis buddies or work colleagues and eventually evolves from there.

There are certain problems that interfere with our relationships with people. These problems need to be dealt with in order to have fruitful relationships.

Healing from hurt

Understanding friendships and relationships is very important because one of the major illnesses prevalent in any General Practice surgery today is depression. Statistics tell us that at any one time 25-40% of all patients registered on a GP list will have some form of depression or mental health disorder. Unfortunately this usually stems out of some form of a dysfunctional relationship. Many people are depressed as a result of how they have been treated by other people in the past. A lot of people have experienced emotional, physical and even sexual abuse. Many are trapped in cycles of abusive relationships where they unconsciously keep seeking out either the perpetrator of abuse or others like those who have abused them.

The Bible clearly tells us that we should help each other to do all we can to live in peace with all men. Hebrews 12:14-17 says

> *God is looking for people to be absorbed into a community where they can experience all that God has for them.*

> Work at living in peace with everyone, and work at living a holy life, for those who are not holy will not see the Lord. Look after each other so that none of you fails to receive the grace of God. Watch out that no poisonous root of bitterness grows up to trouble you, corrupting many. Make sure that no one is immoral or godless like Esau, who traded his birthright as the firstborn son for a single meal. You know that afterward, when he wanted his father's blessing, he was rejected. It was too late for repentance, even though he begged with bitter tears.

When bitterness is allowed to develop for whatever reason it will spread like a wild fire. Bitter people transmit bitterness in the things they say and do which further transmits more bitterness and it can keep on spreading. Hurting people, hurt people. Angry people make people angry. The state of mind we allow ourselves to have, will determine the state of mind we leave others in. That is why the Bible says 'work at living in peace'. It will take effort. Look after each other and watch out because it is very easy to get caught out.

The first step to being healed from the hurts of the past is to forgive. Irrespective of whatever form of abuse has been suffered you need to make the decision to forgive. There are two reasons for this. If you do not forgive, then your own sins will not be forgiven. Mark 11:25 says

> But when you are praying, first forgive anyone you are holding a grudge against, so that your Father in heaven will forgive your sins, too.

Furthermore if you do not forgive you will not be able to move on from the hurt. Every similar occurrence will remind you of it and you will find yourself in the position of hurting other people. Ask God for grace if you are finding it difficult to forgive. Alexander Pope said 'to err is human, to forgive divine'. It takes you drawing on your Christ-like nature to walk in forgiveness.

The second step to being healed from past hurts is to receive healing from God. The Lord wants to heal your broken heart and restore you. He wants to set you free from the prison of depression and hurt. Release your pain to him and let him heal you. Isaiah 61:1 says:

> The Spirit of the Sovereign Lord is upon me, for the Lord has anointed me to bring good news to the poor. He has sent me to comfort the brokenhearted and to proclaim that captives will be released and prisoners will be freed.

The third step may not be necessary but if you are struggling to deal with this on your own then speak to someone mature who you can trust, to pray with you. Matthew 18:19 says:

> I also tell you this: If two of you agree here on earth concerning anything you ask, my Father in heaven will do it for you. For

where two or three gather together as my followers, I am there among them.

When two people agree as touching anything they shall ask God, the Bible tells us He will do it for them. Take the hurts to the Lord in prayer in agreement with a mature believer and the Lord will set you free.

Dealing with Immorality

Immorality can become addictive and many people find themselves caught up in its cycle. If you are having difficulty dealing with this despite your attempts at prayer, then seek help. Find someone you can confide in, an accountability partner, a minister or pastor and pray the prayer of agreement.

Dealing with conflict

What do you do when conflict develops? You may discover that things become frosty between you and someone you once considered a friend. There are scriptural principles and pathways we can follow. Matthew 18:15-17 says:

> If another believer sins against you, go privately and point out the offense. If the other person listens and confesses it, you have won that person back. But if you are unsuccessful, take one or two others with you and go back again, so that everything you say may be confirmed by two or three witnesses. If the person still refuses to listen, take your case to the church. Then if he or she won't accept the church's decision, treat that person as a pagan or a corrupt tax collector.

Matthew 5:22-24 also records:

But I say, if you are even angry with someone, you are subject to judgment! If you call someone an idiot, you are in danger of being brought before the court. And if you curse someone, you are in danger of the fires of hell. "So if you are presenting a sacrifice at the altar in the Temple and you suddenly remember that someone has something against you, leave your sacrifice there at the altar. Go and be reconciled to that person. Then come and offer your sacrifice to God.

The first thing we see from these passages is that you must seek a private audience with the person concerned. Seek to resolve the conflict between the two of you. If this does not resolve things then seek a common friend to help mediate and finally involve church or community leadership, essentially someone you both respect. The most productive means of resolving things is between the two aggrieved parties.

RIGHT QUESTIONS, RIGHT ANSWERS

1. Why is this Decasection important?

This Decasection is important because it looks at your relationship with people as a whole (general), with the opposite sex (gender) and with people whom you have placed in positions of respect (greater). It also helps us to clearly define whom we call our friends and who we should allow to speak into our lives.

2. What must you do to invest in this Decasection of your life? Whatever you do not invest in will depreciate.

Friendships and relationships are like flowers. They need to be looked after, nurtured and encouraged to grow. The five operative words of the definition of a friend will give us clues as to what to do to invest in this area. So you need to spend time with your friends, learn to develop trust in them, be close to them, get to know them better and strengthen your relationship with them.

155

Closing

CLOSING THOUGHTS

This is the conclusion of the matter: God wants us to fear Him and keep His commandments. Understanding the Decasections of Life will enable you to have a grasp on all aspects of life on earth. All areas of life are important to God; that is why He has something to say in His word about all of them.

Ecclesiastes 12:13-14 says:

Here now is my final conclusion: Fear God and obey his commands, for this is everyone's duty. God will judge us for everything we do, including every secret thing, whether good or bad.

My closing thoughts would be to look at the practical applications of the Decasections of Life. There are several:

1. The Decasections help you monitor your progress in life. I developed this concept originally as a means of monitoring my own progress in life. It opened my life up into ten areas which allowed me to review my life periodically to assess how I was doing. This is the prime application. An understanding of the Decasections allows you to review your

life against benchmarks you have set for yourself. Discovering areas in which you are not doing too well will enable you to give some attention and focus to parts of your life which are lacking. It was in the process of sharing with someone on how I use this in my own life, that I realised how useful it could be for others as well.

2. The Decasections enable you to remain motivated. When you reflect and engage in introspection using the Decasections, you are able to clearly see where you are as opposed to where you think you should be. This enables you to remain motivated enough to keep pressing towards your desired goal.

3. The Decasections bring balance to your life. The reason you have ten areas of life is because God has a purpose for all ten. A car has four wheels. Those four wheels are essential for balance. A table has four legs which are likewise essential for balance. You have ten sections and they are all essential for balance. You are not to sacrifice one area of your life for another. Society puts various pressures on people to be successful at work or in church and does not bother if you leave an aspect of your life behind. If your life is imbalanced you can be sure something or someone is suffering somewhere. If you spend too much time working, you may not be having enough time with your family, or in pursuing personal spiritual development or even regular exercise for example.

4. The Decasections of life encourage thanksgiving. I know this personally. Earlier in the book, under the section on Worship, praise and thanksgiving, I gave the example of how Dami and I used the Decasections to encourage worship,

praise and thanksgiving in one of the darkest seasons of our lives. Sometimes when facing challenges we are tempted to think our lives are all about the one or two sore points we are facing. Remember that even when life seems dark, God is always still good and there are probably many other areas which are doing well. Be thankful for these.

5.   The Decasections of life can be used for mentoring. I personally use them as a mentoring tool. When speaking to younger men or youths in general, I usually take them through the Decasections of Life to ensure that they are seeking growth and development in all areas of their lives. Just as you would do for yourself, personal life targets can be set for those being mentored which can later be reviewed.

FINAL THOUGHTS

The Decasections of Life was written by inspiration from God as a service to this generation. The book has a lot of questions and the aim is not necessarily to provide you with all the answers but to kick start meditation, reflection, introspection and self-examination. If however you do have pressing questions about the whole concept of the Decasections, you can email me via my website at *www.decasections.org* and I will be more than willing to tackle any questions you have.

MY PRAYER FOR YOU

I pray that as you have read this book, you will stand perfect and complete in all the will of God for your life. I pray that through the insights you have received, God will grant you peace and rest on every side. I pray that the wisdom you have developed, in reflecting on the material in this book, will cause you to fulfil your purpose in every one of the Decasections of your life in Jesus name. God bless!